To Susan,
May yo[ur]
comfort in [the]
memories of y[our]
mother and in th[e]
inspirational words
herein

Love
Sharen
&
Kelly

Mother Mary

~~~

INSPIRING WORDS
FROM
Pope Francis

~~~

POPE FRANCIS

EDITED BY ALICIA VON STAMWITZ

franciscan
media
Cincinnati, Ohio

Mother Mary is published in collaboration with the Libreria Editrice Vaticana. All excerpts © 2017 Libreria Editrice Vaticana and used by permission.

Cover and book design by Mark Sullivan
Cover image © Giampiero Sposito | Reuters

LIBRARY OF CONGRESS CATALOGING-IN-PUBLICATION DATA
Names: Francis, Pope, 1936- author. | Stamwitz, Alicia von, editor.
Title: Mother Mary : inspiring words from Pope Francis / Pope Francis ; edited by Alicia von Stamwitz.
Description: Cincinnati : Franciscan Media, 2017.
Identifiers: LCCN 2016057327 | ISBN 9781632530561 (hc/jkt)
Subjects: LCSH: Mary, Blessed Virgin, Saint--Quotations. | Catholic Church--Doctrines.
Classification: LCC BX2160.23 .F73 2017 | DDC 232.91--dc23
LC record available at https://lccn.loc.gov/2016057327

ISBN 978-1-63253-056-1

Published by Franciscan Media
28 W. Liberty St.
Cincinnati, OH 45202
www.FranciscanMedia.org

Printed in the United States of America.
Printed on acid-free paper.

17 18 19 20 21   5 4 3 2 1

Contents

INTRODUCTION

Pope Francis has a strong relationship with the Mother of God. As archbishop of Buenos Aires, he encouraged devotion to "Our Lady, Undoer of Knots." On the first day after his election to the papacy, he visited the Basilica of St. Mary Major in Rome to place flowers on the altar and pray for Mary's help and protection. Since that day, he has continued to shine a light on the woman he calls "the first pilgrim" and "the perfect disciple."

When he enters a church or chapel, he often scans the walls and altars for images of Mary. He may approach a painting or statue to study it more closely, touching or kissing it with reverence. Later, he may comment on the Marian art, sharing his personal reflections on the meaning of certain symbols, scenes, or events.

This book gathers Pope Francis's most important and inspiring reflections on God's mother, taken from his own words since becoming the Holy Father. His writings, homilies, prayers, talks, and even tweets are windows not only into Mary's heart, but also into the heart of the pope himself.

For Pope Francis, Mary is an icon of wisdom, strength, courage, and joyful hope. Her unconditional "yes" to God encourages all of us to say "yes" to God's call today. We must turn to Mary often, Pope Francis tells us, for she is a mighty intercessor and a faithful companion on our spiritual journey. Because he highlights Mary's "feminine genius" and her receptivity to divine guidance—something to which believers of various religious traditions aspire—people of many faiths will find nourishment in the pope's words. In his homily of January 1, 2015, he explained, "Mary is so closely united to Jesus because she received from him the knowledge of the heart, the knowledge of faith, nourished by her experience as a mother and by her close relationship with her Son."

Although the chapters and quotations in this collection have been arranged in a certain way, they may be read in any order. Let your curiosity be your guide. Trust it, trust yourself, and trust that the message you most need to hear will find you.

We pray with Pope Francis:

Mary, Mother of Jesus,

you who accepted, teach us how to accept;

you who adored, teach us how to adore;

you who followed, teach us how to follow.

Amen.

—*Alicia von Stamwitz, editor*

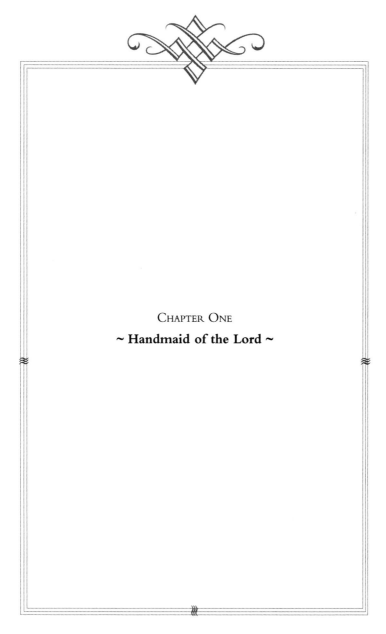

CHAPTER ONE

~ **Handmaid of the Lord** ~

HAIL MARY

On March 25 in the Church, we solemnly celebrate the Annunciation; the mystery of the Incarnation begins. The Archangel Gabriel visits a humble girl in Nazareth and proclaims to her that she will conceive and bear the Son of God. With this Annunciation, the Lord illuminates and strengthens Mary's faith, as he will also do for her spouse, Joseph, so that Jesus could be born into a human family.

This is very beautiful: it shows us how deeply the mystery of the Incarnation, as God desired, encompasses not only conception in the mother's womb, but also acceptance in a real family. Today, I would like to contemplate with you the beauty of this bond, the beauty of God's condescension; and we can do this by reciting the Hail Mary together, the first part of which takes up the words of the angel, those he addressed to the Virgin. I invite you to pray together:

"Hail Mary, full of grace, the Lord is with you. Blessed are you among women, and blessed is the fruit of your womb, Jesus. Holy Mary, Mother of God, pray for us sinners now and at the hour of our death. Amen."

Jesus, Mary and Joseph, in you we contemplate the splendor of true love, to you we turn with trust.

GENERAL AUDIENCE, ST. PETER'S SQUARE,
WEDNESDAY, MARCH 25, 2015

GOD COMES TO DWELL IN US

Mary first conceived Jesus in faith and then in the flesh, when she said "yes" to the message God gave her through the angel. What does this mean? It means that God did not want to become man by bypassing our freedom; he wanted to pass through Mary's free assent, through her "yes." He asked her: "Are you prepared to do this?" And she replied: "Yes."

But what took place most singularly in the Virgin Mary also takes place within us, spiritually, when we receive the Word of God with a good and sincere heart and put it into practice. It is as if God takes flesh within us; he comes to dwell in us, for he dwells in all who love him and keep his word. It is not easy to understand this, but really, it is easy to feel it in our heart.

PRAYER FOR MARIAN DAY, ST. PETER'S SQUARE
SATURDAY, OCTOBER 12, 2013

THE HANDMAID OF THE LORD

The Gospel of St. Luke presents us with Mary, a girl from Nazareth, a small town in Galilee, in the outskirts of the Roman Empire and on the outskirts of Israel as well. A village. Yet the Lord's gaze rested on her, on this little girl from that distant village, on the one he had chosen to be the Mother of his Son. In view of this motherhood, Mary was preserved from original sin, from that fracture in communion with God, with others and with creation, which deeply wounds every human being. But this fracture was healed in advance in the Mother of the One who came to free us from the slavery of sin. The *Immaculata* was written in God's design; she is the fruit of God's love that saves the world.

And Our Lady never distanced herself from that love: throughout her life her whole being is a "yes" to that love, it is the "yes" to God. But that didn't make life easy for her! When the angel calls her "full of grace" (Luke 1:28), she is "greatly troubled" for, in her humility, she feels she is nothing before God. The angel consoles her: "Do not be afraid, Mary, for you have found favor with God. And behold, you will conceive in your womb and bear a son, and you shall call his name Jesus" (v. 30, 31). This announcement troubles her even more because she was not yet married to Joseph; but the angel adds: "The Holy Spirit will come upon you...therefore the child to be born will be called holy, the Son of God" (v. 35). Mary listens, interiorly obeys, and responds: "Behold, I am the handmaid of the Lord; let it be done to me according to your word" (v. 38).

ANGELUS, ST. PETER'S SQUARE
SUNDAY, DECEMBER 8, 2013, SOLEMNITY OF THE
IMMACULATE CONCEPTION

THE HUMBLE WOMAN OF NAZARETH

On this first day of the year, in the joyful—albeit cold—atmosphere of Christmas, the Church invites us to fix our gaze of faith and of love on the Mother of Jesus. In her, the humble woman of Nazareth, "the Word became flesh and made his dwelling among us" (John 1:14). Because of this it is impossible to separate contemplating Jesus, the Word of Life who has become visible and tangible (cf. 1 John 1:1), from contemplating Mary, who has given him her love and his human flesh.

ANGELUS, ST. PETER'S SQUARE
THURSDAY, JANUARY 1, 2015, SOLEMNITY OF MARY,
MOTHER OF GOD

Pope Francis @Pontifex · August 15, 2015
Mary's life shows that God accomplishes great deeds through those who are the most humble.

JESUS IS COMING!

Mary teaches us to seize the right moment when Jesus comes into our life and asks for a ready and generous answer. And Jesus is coming. Indeed, the mystery of the birth of Jesus in Bethlehem took place historically more than 2,000 years ago but occurs as a spiritual event in the "today" of the Liturgy. The Word, who found a home in the virgin womb of Mary, comes in the celebration of Christmas to knock once again at the heart of every Christian. He comes and knocks. Each of us is called to respond, like Mary, with a personal and sincere "yes," placing oneself fully at the disposal of God and of his mercy, of his love.

How many times Jesus comes into our lives, and how many times he sends us an angel, and how many times we don't notice because we are so taken, immersed in our own thoughts, in our own affairs and even, in these days, in our Christmas preparations, so as not to notice him who comes and knocks at the door of our hearts, asking for acceptance, asking for a "yes" like Mary's.

ANGELUS, ST. PETER'S SQUARE
SUNDAY, DECEMBER 21, 2014

EVERYTHING IS GRACE

The message of today's Solemnity of the Immaculate Conception of the Virgin Mary can be summed up in these words: everything is a free gift from God, everything is grace, everything is a gift out of his love for us. The angel Gabriel calls Mary "full of grace" (Luke 1:28): in her there is no room for sin, because God chose her from eternity to be the Mother of Jesus and preserved her from original sin. And Mary corresponds to the grace and abandons herself, saying to the angel: "Let it be done to me according to your word" (Luke 38). She does not say: "I shall do it according to your word." No! But: "Let it be done to me…." And the Word was made flesh in her womb.

ANGELUS, ST. PETER'S SQUARE
MONDAY, DECEMBER 8, 2014, SOLEMNITY OF THE
IMMACULATE CONCEPTION

Pope Francis @Pontifex · December 30, 2013

Our Mother Mary is full of beauty because she is full of grace.

A LUMINOUS EVENT

The Angelus prayer is a beautiful popular expression of the faith. It is a simple prayer, recited at three specific times during the day. It thus punctuates the rhythm of our daily activities: in the morning, at midday, and at sunset. But it is an important prayer. I encourage each of you to recite it, along with the Hail Mary. It reminds us of a luminous event which transformed history: the Incarnation, the moment when the Son of God became man in Jesus of Nazareth.

ANGELUS, ARCHBISHOP'S RESIDENCE,
ST. JOAQUIN, RIO DE JANIERO, BRAZIL
FRIDAY, JULY 26, 2013

TRANSFORMED BY LOVE

The mystery of this girl from Nazareth, who is in the heart of God, is not estranged from us. She is not there and we over here. No, we are connected. Indeed, God rests his loving gaze on every man and every woman! By name and surname. His gaze of love is on every one of us....

On this solemnity, then, by contemplating our beautiful Immaculate Mother, let us also recognize our truest destiny, our deepest vocation: to be loved, to be transformed by love, to be transformed by the beauty of God. Let us look to her, our Mother, and allow her to look upon us, for she is our Mother and she loves us so much; let us allow ourselves to be watched over by her so that we may learn how to be more humble, and also more courageous in following the Word of God; to welcome the tender embrace of her Son Jesus, an embrace that gives us life, hope and peace.

ANGELUS, ST. PETER'S SQUARE
SUNDAY, DECEMBER 8, 2013, SOLEMNITY OF THE
IMMACULATE CONCEPTION

MARY IS CLOSE TO US

The Mother of God. This is the first and most important title of Our Lady. It refers to a quality, a role which the faith of the Christian people, in its tender and genuine devotion to our heavenly Mother, has understood from the beginning....

Mary has always been present in the hearts, the piety and above all the pilgrimage of faith of the Christian people. "The Church journeys through time...and on this journey she proceeds along the path already trodden by the Virgin Mary" (*Redemptoris Mater*, 2). Our journey of faith is the same as that of Mary, and so we feel that she is particularly close to us.

HOMILY, VATICAN BASILICA,
WEDNESDAY, JANUARY 1, 2014, SOLEMNITY OF MARY,
MOTHER OF GOD

WE MUST IMITATE MARY

St. Luke says that Mary, with Jesus in her womb, arose and went in haste to serve her cousin Elizabeth who, in her old age, was about to become a mother (cf. Luke 1:39–45). She did God's will by making herself available to those who needed her. She did not think of herself; she overcame adversity and gave herself to others.

Victory is for those who continually arise without being discouraged. If we imitate Mary, we cannot keep our arms folded, only complaining, or perhaps dodging the hard work that others do and which is our responsibility. This is not about doing great things, but about doing everything with tenderness and mercy.

Mary was always with her people supporting the least. She knew loneliness, poverty and exile, and she learned to create fraternity and to make her home in any place where goodness took root. Let us beseech her to give us a poor spirit which is not proud, a pure heart that sees God in the face of the neediest, and great patience that we may not shrink when confronted with life's difficulties.

MESSAGE TO THE CUBAN EPISCOPAL CONFERENCE,
FROM THE VATICAN
MONDAY, SEPTEMBER 8, 2014

MARY'S "YES"

We have just heard how Mary went to meet her cousin Elizabeth. She set out without delay, without doubts, without lessening her pace, to be with her relative who was in the last months of her pregnancy.

Mary's encounter with the angel did not hold her back since she did not consider herself privileged, or make her hesitate in leaving those around her. On the contrary, it renewed and inspired an attitude for which Mary is and always will be known: she is the woman who says "yes," a "yes" of surrender to God and, at the same time, a "yes" of surrender to her brothers and sisters.

HOMILY, BASILICA OF OUR LADY OF GUADALUPE,
MEXICO CITY
SATURDAY, FEBRUARY 12, 2016

Pope Francis @Pontifex · April 23, 2013
Mary is the one who says "yes." Mary, help us to come to know the voice of Jesus better, and to follow it.

BLESSED AMONG WOMEN

Today, we are reminded of the words of blessing which Elizabeth spoke to the Virgin Mary: "Blessed are you among women, and blessed is the fruit of your womb! And why has this happened to me, that the mother of my Lord comes to me?" (Luke 1:42–43).

This blessing is in continuity with the priestly blessing which God had given to Moses to be passed on to Aaron and to all the people: "The Lord bless you and keep you; the Lord make his face to shine upon you and be gracious to you; the Lord lift up his countenance upon you, and give you peace" (Numbers 6:24–26). In celebrating the Solemnity of Mary Most Holy, the Holy Mother of God, the Church reminds us that Mary, more than anyone else, received this blessing. In her, the blessing finds fulfillment, for no other creature has ever seen God's face shine upon it as did Mary. She gave a human face to the eternal Word, so that all of us can contemplate him.

HOMILY, VATICAN BASILICA
THURSDAY, JANUARY 1, 2015, SOLEMNITY OF MARY,
MOTHER OF GOD

HASTEN OUR STEPS TO BETHLEHEM

May the Virgin Mary help us to hasten our steps to Bethlehem, to encounter the Child who is born for us, for the salvation and joy of all people. To her the angel said: "Hail, full of grace: the Lord is with you" (Luke 1:28). May she obtain for us the grace to live the joy of the Gospel in our families, at work, in the parish and everywhere. An intimate joy, fashioned of wonder and tenderness. The joy a mother experiences when she looks at her newborn baby and feels that he or she is a gift from God, a miracle for which she can give only thanks!

ANGELUS, ST. PETER'S SQUARE
THIRD SUNDAY OF ADVENT, DECEMBER 15, 2013

GOD HAS DONE MARVELOUS THINGS!
In the Psalm we said: "Sing to the Lord a new song, for he has done marvelous things" (Psalm 98:1).

Today we consider one of the marvelous things which the Lord has done: Mary! A lowly and weak creature like ourselves, she was chosen to be the Mother of God, the Mother of her Creator....

At the message of the angel, she does not hide her surprise. It is the astonishment of realizing that God, to become man, had chosen her, a simple maid of Nazareth; not someone who lived in a palace amid power and riches, or one who had done extraordinary things, but simply someone who was open to God and put her trust in him, even without understanding everything: "Here I am, the servant of the Lord; let it be with me according to your word" (Luke 1:38). That was her answer.

HOMILY FOR MARIAN DAY, ST. PETER'S SQUARE
SUNDAY, OCTOBER 13, 2013

A FAITH WHICH UNITES US

I would like to think for a moment about Joseph and Mary in Bethlehem. They were forced to leave home, families and friends. They had to leave all that they had and they had to go somewhere else, to a place where they knew no one, a place where they had no house, no family. That was when that young couple had Jesus. That was how, having made preparations as best they could in a cave, they gave us Jesus. They were alone, in a strange land, just the three of them. Then, all of a sudden, people began to appear: shepherds, people just like them who had to leave their homes to find better opportunities for their families....

I come to you here like those shepherds who went to Bethlehem. I want to be your neighbor. I want to bless your faith, your hands and your community. I come to join you in giving thanks, because faith has become hope, and hope in turn kindles love.... This is the faith which unites us in solidarity, it unites us to our elder brother, Jesus, and our Mother, the Blessed Virgin.

ADDRESS TO THE PEOPLE OF BAÑADO NORTE,
ASUNCIÓN, PARAGUAY
SUNDAY, JULY 12, 2015

A SIGN OF HOPE

Let us always have at heart the Virgin Mary, a humble girl from small people lost on the fringes of a great empire, a homeless mother who could turn a stable for beasts into a home for Jesus with just a few swaddling clothes and much tenderness. Mary is a sign of hope for peoples suffering the birth pangs of justice.

ADDRESS, WORLD MEETING OF POPULAR MOVEMENTS,
SANTA CRUZ DE LA SIERRA, BOLIVIA
THURSDAY, JULY 9, 2015

CONTEMPLATING THE NATIVITY SCENE

Isaiah's prophecy announces the rising of a great light which breaks through the night. This light is born in Bethlehem and is welcomed by the loving arms of Mary, by the love of Joseph, by the wonder of the shepherds....

The question put to us simply by the Infant's presence is: Do I allow God to love me?...

Dear brothers and sisters, on this holy night we contemplate the Nativity scene: there "the people who walked in darkness have seen a great light" (Isaiah 9:1). People who were unassuming, people open to receiving the gift of God, were the ones who saw this light. This light was not seen, however, by the arrogant, the proud, by those who made laws according to their own personal measures, who were closed off to others. Let us look to the crib and pray, asking the Blessed Mother: "O Mary, show us Jesus!"

HOMILY, MIDNIGHT MASS, VATICAN BASILICA
WEDNESDAY, DECEMBER 24, 2014, SOLEMNITY OF THE
NATIVITY OF THE LORD

MARY PRESENTS JESUS TO THE WORLD

In these days, the Church's liturgy sets before our eyes the icon of the Virgin Mary, Mother of God. The first day of the year is the feast of the Mother of God, followed by the Epiphany, commemorating the visit of the Magi. The Evangelist Matthew writes: "Going into the house they saw the child with Mary, his Mother, and they fell down and worshipped him" (Matthew 2:11). It is the Mother who, after giving birth to him, presents the Son to the world. She gives us Jesus, she shows us Jesus, she lets us see Jesus.

GENERAL AUDIENCE, PAUL VI AUDIENCE HALL,
WEDNESDAY, JANUARY 7, 2015

AN ICON OF LOVE

The Baby Jesus with his Mother Mary and with St. Joseph are a simple but so luminous icon of the family. The light it casts is the light of mercy and salvation for all the world, the light of truth for every man, for the human family and for individual families. This light which comes from the Holy Family encourages us to offer human warmth in those family situations in which, for various reasons, peace is lacking, harmony is lacking, and forgiveness is lacking. May our concrete solidarity not diminish, especially with regard to the families who are experiencing more difficult situations due to illness, unemployment, discrimination, the need to emigrate....

Let us entrust to Mary, Queen and Mother of the family, all the families of the world, that they may live in faith, in accord, in reciprocal aid; and, for this, I invoke upon them the maternal protection of the One who was the mother and daughter of her Son.

ANGELUS, ST. PETER'S SQUARE
SUNDAY, DECEMBER 28, 2014, FEAST OF THE HOLY FAMILY

THE MOTHER OF OUR REDEEMER

The Holy Year will open on December 8, 2015, the Solemnity of the Immaculate Conception. This liturgical feast day recalls God's action from the very beginning of the history of mankind. After the sin of Adam and Eve, God did not wish to leave humanity alone in the throes of evil. And so he turned his gaze to Mary, holy and immaculate in love (cf. Ephesians 1:4), choosing her to be the Mother of man's Redeemer.

MISERICORDIAE VULTUS (PAPAL BULL ON THE
EXTRAORDINARY JUBILEE OF MERCY), 3
SATURDAY, APRIL 11, 2015

READY OURSELVES TO CELEBRATE

Let us make ourselves ready to celebrate Christmas by contemplating Mary and Joseph: Mary, the woman full of grace who had the courage to entrust herself totally to the Word of God; Joseph, the faithful and just man who chose to believe the Lord rather than listen to the voices of doubt and human pride. With them, let us walk together toward Bethlehem.

ANGELUS, ST. PETER'S SQUARE
FOURTH SUNDAY OF ADVENT, DECEMBER 22, 2013

TEACH US TO WELCOME GOD MADE MAN

What shall we do, how shall we act in the coming year in order to make our city a little better?…

Let us give thanks for all the blessings which God has bestowed on us, especially for his patience and his faithfulness, which are manifest over the course of time, but in a singular way in the fullness of time, when "God sent forth his Son, born of woman" (Galatians 4:4). May the Mother of God, in whose name tomorrow we begin a new phase of our earthly pilgrimage, teach us to welcome God made man, so that every year, every month, every day may be filled with his eternal Love. So be it!

HOMILY, VATICAN BASILICA
TUESDAY, DECEMBER 31, 2013

OUR COMMON HORIZON

Just as in each of our lives, we always need to begin again, to get up again, to rediscover the meaning of the goal of our lives, so also for the great human family it is always necessary to rediscover the common horizon toward which we are journeying....

The model of this spiritual disposition, of this way of being and journeying in life, is the Virgin Mary. A simple girl from the country who carries within her heart the fullness of hope in God! In her womb, God's hope took flesh, it became man, it became history: Jesus Christ. Her Magnificat is the canticle of the People of God on a journey, and of all men and women who hope in God and in the power of his mercy. Let us allow ourselves to be guided by her, she who is Mother, a *Mamma,* and knows how to guide us. Let us allow ourselves to be guided by her during this season of active waiting and watchfulness.

ANGELUS, ST. PETER'S SQUARE
FIRST SUNDAY OF ADVENT, DECEMBER 1, 2013

Pope Francis @Pontifex · February 13, 2016

Mary is the woman who says "yes," a "yes" of surrender to God, a "yes" of surrender to her brothers and sisters. May we follow her example.

HELP US TO RECEIVE JESUS

May the Holy Virgin, the Holy Mother of God, who was at the very heart of the temple of God, when the Word— who was in the beginning—made himself one with us in time; may she who gave the Savior to the world, help us to receive him with an open heart, in order that we may truly be and live freely, as children of God.

HOMILY, VATICAN BASILICA
WEDNESDAY, DECEMBER 31, 2014

SING WITH MARY

All of us, together with the poor of the earth, can sing with Mary: "He has put down the mighty from their thrones, and exalted those of low degree; he has filled the hungry with good things, and the rich he has sent empty away" (Luke 1:52–53).

GENERAL AUDIENCE, ST. PETER'S SQUARE
WEDNESDAY, MAY 18, 2016

CHAPTER TWO

~ Model of Faith ~

A SHARED PILGRIMAGE

As far as faith, the hinge of the Christian life, is concerned, the Mother of God shared our condition. She had to take the same path as ourselves, a path which is sometimes difficult and obscure. She had to advance in the "pilgrimage of faith." Our pilgrimage of faith has been inseparably linked to Mary ever since Jesus, dying on the cross, gave her to us as our Mother, saying: "Behold your Mother!" (John 19:27).

HOMILY, VATICAN BASILICA,
WEDNESDAY, JANUARY 1, 2014, SOLEMNITY OF MARY,
MOTHER OF GOD

MOTHER AND DISCIPLE

Let us contemplate the one who knew and loved Jesus like no other creature. The Gospel that we heard reveals the fundamental way Mary expressed her love for Jesus: by doing the will of God.

"For whoever does the will of my Father in heaven is my brother, and sister, and mother" (Matthew 12:50). With these words Jesus leaves us an important message: the will of God is the supreme law which establishes true belonging to him. That is how Mary established a bond of kinship with Jesus even before giving birth to him.

She becomes both disciple and Mother to the Son at the moment she receives the words of the angel and says: "Behold, I am the handmaid of the Lord; let it be done to me according to your word" (Luke 1:38). This "let it be" is not only acceptance, but also a trustful openness to the future. This "let it be" is hope!

ADDRESS TO THE CAMALDOLESE
BENEDICTINE NUNS, ROME
THURSDAY, NOVEMBER 21, 2013

MARY, TEACH US

Mary, Mother of Jesus,

you who accepted, teach us how to accept;

you who adored, teach us how to adore;

you who followed, teach us how to follow. Amen.

HOMILY, MANGER SQUARE, BETHLEHEM
SUNDAY, MAY 25, 2014

DO WHATEVER JESUS TELLS YOU

Dear friends, we have come to knock at the door of Mary's house. She has opened it for us, she has let us in and she shows us her Son. Now she asks us to "do whatever he tells you" (John 2:5). Yes, Mother, we are committed to doing whatever Jesus tells us! And we will do it with hope, trusting in God's surprises and full of joy. Amen.

HOMILY, BASILICA OF THE SHRINE OF
OUR LADY OF APARECIDA, BRAZIL
WEDNESDAY, JULY 24, 2013

ABANDONED TO LOVE

The Archangel Gabriel reveals to the Virgin the Lord's will that she become the Mother of his only-begotten Son....

Responding to the angel, Mary said: "Behold, I am the handmaid of the Lord; let it be to me according to your word" (v. 38). In her "behold" filled with faith, Mary does not know by what road she must venture, what pains she must suffer, what risks she must face. But she is aware that it is the Lord asking and she entrusts herself totally to him; she abandons herself to his love. This is the faith of Mary!

ANGELUS, ST. PETER'S SQUARE,
SUNDAY, DECEMBER 21, 2014

Pope Francis @Pontifex · May 18, 2013
We must learn from Mary, and we must imitate her unconditional readiness to receive Christ in her life.

INVITED TO SERVE

In the Gospel, the Lord invites us to accept our mission without placing conditions. It is an important message which we must never forget. Here, in this sanctuary dedicated to Our Lady of the Presentation, it resounds in a special way. Mary is an example of discipleship for us who, like her, have received a vocation. Her trusting response, "Be it done unto me according to your word," reminds us of her words at the wedding feast of Cana: "Do whatever he tells you" (John 2:5). Her example is an invitation to serve as she served.

ADDRESS TO CLERGY, RELIGIOUS AND SEMINARIANS,
QUITO, ECUADOR
WEDNESDAY, JULY 8, 2015

CAPABLE OF MAKING A COMMITMENT

Mary as a good mother teaches us to be, like her, capable of making definitive decisions; definitive choices, at this moment in a time controlled by, so to speak, a philosophy of the provisional. It is very difficult to make a lifetime commitment. And she helps us to make those definitive decisions in the full freedom with which she said "yes" to the plan God had for her life (cf. Luke 1:38).

RECITAL OF THE HOLY ROSARY, BASILICA OF
ST. MARY MAJOR, ROME
SATURDAY, MAY 4, 2013

Pope Francis @Pontifex · August 31, 2013
Let us ask Mary to help us fix our eyes intently on Jesus, to follow him always, even if this is demanding.

WE ARE ALL BEARERS OF CHRIST

The Feast of the Immaculate Conception then becomes the feast of all of us if, with our daily "yes," we manage to overcome our selfishness and make the life of our brothers ever more glad, to give them hope, by drying a few tears and giving a bit of joy. In imitation of Mary, we are called to become bearers of Christ and witnesses to his love, looking first of all to those who are privileged in the eyes of Jesus. It is they who he himself indicated: "I was hungry and you gave me food, I was thirsty and you gave me drink, I was a stranger and you welcomed me, I was naked and you clothed me, I was sick and you visited me, I was in prison and you came to me" (Matthew 25:35–36).

ANGELUS, ST. PETER'S SQUARE
TUESDAY, DECEMBER 8, 2015, SOLEMNITY OF THE
IMMACULATE CONCEPTION

RECEIVE THE HOLY SPIRIT

The attitude of Mary of Nazareth shows us that *being* comes before *doing*, and *to leave the doing* to God in order *to be* truly as he wants us. It is he who works so many marvels in us. Mary is receptive, but not passive. Because, on the physical level, she receives the power of the Holy Spirit and then gives flesh and blood to the Son of God who forms within her. Thus, on the spiritual level, she accepts the grace and corresponds to it with faith. That is why St. Augustine affirms that the Virgin "conceived in her heart before her womb" (*Discourses*, 215, 4). She conceived first faith and then the Lord. This mystery of the acceptance of grace, which in Mary, as a unique privilege, was without the obstacle of sin, is a possibility for all.

ANGELUS, ST. PETER'S SQUARE
MONDAY, DECEMBER 8, 2014, SOLEMNITY OF THE
IMMACULATE CONCEPTION

Pope Francis @Pontifex · December 6, 2014

Advent begins a new journey. May Mary, our Mother, be our guide.

SAFE IN GOD'S HANDS

Nothing and no one can take us from the hands of Jesus, because nothing and no one can overcome his love. Jesus's love is invincible. The evil one, the great enemy of God and of his creatures, attempts in many ways to take eternal life from us. But the evil one can do nothing if we ourselves do not open the doors of our hearts to him, by following his deceitful enticements.

The Virgin Mary heard and obediently followed the voice of the Good Shepherd. May she help us to welcome with joy Jesus's invitation to become his disciples, and to always live in the certainty of being in the paternal hands of the Father.

REGINA COELI, ST. PETER'S SQUARE
SUNDAY, APRIL 17, 2016

NOURISHED BY THE WORD OF GOD

For the faith to respond, to avoid being suffocated, it must be constantly nourished by the Word of God.... The model is the Virgin Mary, who, St. Luke tells us, pondered in her heart the words and events concerning her Son Jesus (cf. Luke 2:19). May Our Lady teach us to welcome the Word of God fully, not only through intellectual research, but in our whole life.

ADDRESS TO THE ITALIAN BIBLICAL ASSOCIATION,
CLEMENTINE HALL,
FRIDAY, SEPTEMBER 12, 2014

WE ARE CALLED TO GIVE FREELY

As we have received freely, so are we called to give freely (cf. Matthew 10:8); imitating Mary, who, immediately upon receiving the angel's announcement, went to share the gift of her fruitfulness with her relative Elizabeth. Because if everything has been given to us, then everything must be passed on. How? By allowing that the Holy Spirit make of us a gift for others.

ANGELUS, ST. PETER'S SQUARE
MONDAY, DECEMBER 8, 2014, SOLEMNITY OF THE
IMMACULATE CONCEPTION

LIVING OUR FAITH LIKE MARY

In what sense does Mary represent a model for the Church's faith? Let us think about who the Virgin Mary was: a Jewish girl who was waiting with all her heart for the redemption of her people....

Mary's faith is the fulfillment of Israel's faith; the whole journey, the whole path of that people awaiting redemption, is contained in her, and it is in this sense that she is the model of the Church's faith, which has Christ, the incarnation of God's infinite love, as its center.

How did Mary live this faith? She lived it out in the simplicity of the thousand daily tasks and worries of every mother, such as providing food, clothing, caring for the house.... It was precisely Our Lady's normal life which served as the basis for the unique relationship and profound dialogue which unfolded between her and God, between her and her Son. Mary's "yes," already perfect from the start, grew until the hour of the Cross. There her motherhood opened to embrace every one of us, our lives, so as to guide us to her Son.

GENERAL AUDIENCE, ST. PETER'S SQUARE
WEDNESDAY, OCTOBER 23, 2013

STRIVE EVER HIGHER

The Gospel of St. Luke tells us that, in the family of Nazareth, Jesus "grew and became strong, filled with wisdom; and the favor of God was upon him" (Luke 2:40). Our Lady does just this for us, she helps us to grow as human beings and in the faith, to be strong and never to fall into the temptation of being human beings and Christians in a superficial way, but to live responsibly, to strive ever higher.

RECITAL OF THE HOLY ROSARY,
BASILICA OF ST. MARY MAJOR
SATURDAY, MAY 4, 2013

HELP US TO KNOW JESUS'S VOICE

Today's passage records these words of Jesus: "My sheep hear my voice, and I know them, and they follow me; and I give them eternal life, and they shall never perish, and no one shall snatch them out of my hand. My Father, who has given them to me is greater than all, and no one is able to snatch them out of the Father's hand. I and the Father are one" (John 10:27–30). These four verses contain the whole of Jesus's message; it is the nucleus of his Gospel: he calls us to share in his relationship with the Father, and this is eternal life....

Let us invoke the intercession of Mary who is the Woman of the "yes." Mary said "yes" throughout her life! She learned to recognize Jesus's voice from the time when she carried him in her womb. May Mary, our Mother, help us to know Jesus's voice better and better and to follow it, so as to walk on the path of life!...

Let us all pray together to Our Lady.

REGINA COELI, ST. PETER'S SQUARE
SUNDAY, APRIL 21, 2013

KNOWLEDGE OF THE HEART

Mary is so closely united to Jesus because she received from him the knowledge of the heart, the knowledge of faith, nourished by her experience as a mother and by her close relationship with her Son. The Blessed Virgin is the woman of faith who made room for God in her heart and in her plans; she is the believer capable of perceiving in the gift of her Son the coming of that "fullness of time" (Galatians 4:4) in which God, by choosing the humble path of human existence, entered personally into the history of salvation. That is why Jesus cannot be understood without his Mother.

HOMILY, VATICAN BASILICA
THURSDAY, JANUARY 1, 2015, SOLEMNITY OF MARY,
MOTHER OF GOD

Pope Francis @Pontifex · August 14, 2016

We ask Mary, our Mother, to help us to pray with a humble heart.

THE MYSTERIES OF JESUS

In the Gospels, St. Luke twice emphasizes the attitude of Mary, which is also that of St. Joseph: she "kept all these things, pondering them in her heart" (Luke 2:19, 51). To listen to the Lord, we must learn to contemplate, to feel his constant presence in our lives, and we must stop and converse with him, give him space in prayer....

And in this month of May, I would like to recall the importance and beauty of the prayer of the Holy Rosary. Reciting the Hail Mary, we are led to contemplate the mysteries of Jesus, that is, to reflect on the key moments of his life, so that, as with Mary and St. Joseph, he is the center of our thoughts, of our attention and our actions....

Dear brothers and sisters, let us ask St. Joseph and the Virgin Mary to teach us to be faithful to our daily tasks, to live our faith in the actions of everyday life, and to give more space to the Lord in our lives, to pause to contemplate his face.

GENERAL AUDIENCE, ST. PETER'S SQUARE
WEDNESDAY, MAY 1, 2013

A SIMPLE CONTEMPLATIVE PRAYER

Here I would like to emphasize the beauty of a simple contemplative prayer, accessible to all, great and small, the educated and those with little education. It is the prayer of the Holy Rosary.

In the Rosary we turn to the Virgin Mary so that she may guide us to an ever closer union with her Son Jesus to bring us into conformity with him, to have his sentiments and to behave like him. Indeed, in the Rosary while we repeat the Hail Mary we meditate on the Mysteries, on the events of Christ's life, so as to know and love him ever better. The Rosary is an effective means for opening ourselves to God, for it helps us to overcome egotism and to bring peace to hearts, in the family, in society and in the world.

MESSAGE TO YOUNG LITHUANIANS,
FROM THE VATICAN
FRIDAY, JUNE 21, 2013

SPIRITUAL MEDICINE

Now I would like to recommend a medicine to you. Some of you may be wondering: "Is the Pope a pharmacist now?" It is a special medicine which will help you to benefit from the Year of Faith, as it soon will come to an end. It is a medicine that consists of 59 threaded beads; a "spiritual medicine" called *Misericordin*. A small box containing 59 beads on a string. This little box contains the medicine, and it will be distributed to you by volunteers as you leave the square.

Take them! There is a Rosary, with which you can pray the Chaplet of Divine Mercy, spiritual help for our souls and for spreading love, forgiveness, and brotherhood everywhere. Do not forget to take it, because it is good for you. It is good for the heart, the soul, and for life in general!

ANGELUS, ST. PETER'S SQUARE
SUNDAY, NOVEMBER 17, 2013

ULTIMATE FIDELITY

Mary said her "yes" to God: a "yes" which threw her simple life in Nazareth into turmoil, and not only once. Any number of times she had to utter a heartfelt "yes" at moments of joy and sorrow, culminating in the "yes" she spoke at the foot of the Cross. Here today there are many mothers present; think of the full extent of Mary's faithfulness to God: seeing her only Son hanging on the Cross. The faithful woman, still standing, utterly heartbroken, yet faithful and strong.

And I ask myself: Am I a Christian by fits and starts, or am I a Christian full-time? Our culture of the ephemeral, the relative, also takes its toll on the way we live our faith. God asks us to be faithful to him, daily, in our everyday life. He goes on to say that, even if we are sometimes unfaithful to him, he remains faithful. In his mercy, he never tires of stretching out his hand to lift us up, to encourage us to continue our journey, to come back and tell him of our weakness, so that he can grant us his strength. This is the real journey: to walk with the Lord always, even at moments of weakness, even in our sins. Never to prefer a makeshift path of our own. That kills us. Faith is ultimate fidelity, like that of Mary.

HOMILY, MARIAN DAY, ST. PETER'S SQUARE
SUNDAY, OCTOBER 13, 2013

A FLAME BURNING IN THE NIGHT

Mary was always with Jesus, she followed Jesus in the midst of the crowds and she heard all the gossip and the nastiness of those who opposed the Lord. And she carried this cross! Mary's faith encountered misunderstanding and contempt. When Jesus's "hour" came, the hour of his passion, when Mary's faith was a little flame burning in the night, a little light flickering in the darkness, through the night of Holy Saturday, Mary kept watch. Her flame, small but bright, remained burning until the dawn of the Resurrection. And when she received word that the tomb was empty, her heart was filled with the joy of faith: Christian faith in the death and Resurrection of Jesus Christ.... What is our faith like? Like Mary, do we keep it burning even at times of difficulty, in moments of darkness? Do I feel the joy of faith?

PRAYER FOR MARIAN DAY, ST. PETER'S SQUARE
SATURDAY, OCTOBER 12, 2013

THE FIRST AND PERFECT DISCIPLE

Holy Saturday is the day on which the Church contemplates the "repose" of Christ in the sepulcher after the victorious battle of the Cross. On Holy Saturday, the Church, yet again, identifies with Mary: all her faith is gathered in her, the first and perfect disciple, the first and perfect believer. In the darkness that enveloped creation, she alone stayed to keep the flame of faith burning, hoping against all hope (cf. Romans 4:18) in the Resurrection of Jesus.

GENERAL AUDIENCE, ST. PETER'S SQUARE
WEDNESDAY, APRIL 1, 2015

A FAITHFUL WITNESS

The silent witness to the events of Jesus's Passion and Resurrection was Mary. She stood beside the Cross: she did not fold in the face of pain; her faith made her strong. In the broken heart of the Mother, the flame of hope was kept ever burning. Let us ask her to help us too to fully accept the Easter proclamation of the Resurrection, so as to embody it in the concreteness of our daily lives.

May the Virgin Mary give us the faithful certitude that every step suffered on our journey, illuminated by the light of Easter, will become a blessing and a joy for us and for others, especially for those suffering because of selfishness and indifference.

REGINA COELI, ST. PETER'S SQUARE
EASTER MONDAY, MARCH 28, 2016

IN UNION WITH JESUS

The life of the Holy Virgin was the life of a woman of her people: Mary prayed, she worked, she went to the synagogue.... But every action was carried out in perfect union with Jesus. This union finds its culmination on Calvary: here Mary is united to the Son in the martyrdom of her heart and in the offering of his life to the Father for the salvation of humanity. Our Lady shared in the pain of the Son and accepted with him the will of the Father, in that obedience that bears fruit, that grants the true victory over evil and death.

The reality Mary teaches us is very beautiful: to always be united with Jesus.

GENERAL AUDIENCE, ST. PETER'S SQUARE
WEDNESDAY, OCTOBER 23, 2013

INSTRUMENTS IN GOD'S HANDS

Do we think that Jesus's incarnation is simply a past event which has nothing to do with us personally? Believing in Jesus means giving him our flesh with the humility and courage of Mary, so that he can continue to dwell in our midst. It means giving him our hands, to caress the little ones and the poor; our feet, to go forth and meet our brothers and sisters; our arms, to hold up the weak and to work in the Lord's vineyard; our minds, to think and act in the light of the Gospel; and, especially, to offer our hearts to love and to make choices in accordance with God's will. All this happens thanks to the working of the Holy Spirit. And in this way we become instruments in God's hands, so that Jesus can act in the world through us.

PRAYER FOR MARIAN DAY, ST. PETER'S SQUARE
SATURDAY, OCTOBER 12, 2013

Pope Francis @Pontifex · June 3, 2013
Sometimes we know what we have to do, but we lack the courage to do it. Let us learn from Mary how to make decisions, trusting in the Lord.

WITH OUR GAZE FIXED ON JESUS

"Blessed is she who believed!" Mary is blessed for her faith in God, for her faith, because her heart's gaze was always fixed on God, the Son of God whom she bore in her womb and whom she contemplated upon the Cross. In the adoration of the Blessed Sacrament, Mary says to us: "Look at my son Jesus, keep your gaze fixed on him, listen to him, speak with him. He is gazing at you with love. Do not be afraid! He will teach you to follow him and to bear witness to him in all that you do, whether great and small, in your family life, at work, at times of celebration. He will teach you to go out of yourself and to look upon others with love, as he did. He loved you and loves you, not with words but with deeds."

O Mary, let us feel your maternal gaze. Guide us to your Son. May we not be Christians "on display," but Christians ready to "get our hands dirty" in building, with your Son Jesus, his Kingdom of love, joy and peace.

VIDEO MESSAGE FOR PRAYER VIGIL AT THE SHRINE OF
DIVINE LOVE, FROM THE VATICAN
SATURDAY, OCTOBER 12, 2013

OUR LADY'S LEGACY

The words Mary addresses to the servants come to crown the wedding of Cana: "Do whatever he tells you" (John 2:5). It is curious: these are her last words recounted by the Gospels: they are the legacy that she hands down to us. Today too Our Lady says to us all: "Whatever he tells you—Jesus tells you—do it." It is the legacy that she has left us: it is beautiful!…

To serve the Lord means to listen and to put into practice his Word. It is the simple but essential recommendation of the Mother of Jesus and it is the program of life of the Christian.

GENERAL AUDIENCE, ST. PETER'S SQUARE
WEDNESDAY, JUNE 8, 2016

MARY, HELP US WALK IN LOVE

Today's liturgy presents us with the parable of the "Good Samaritan," taken from the Gospel of Luke (10:25–37). This passage, this simple and inspiring story, indicates a way of life, which has as its main point not ourselves, but others, with their difficulties, whom we encounter on our journey and who challenge us. Others challenge us. And when others do not challenge us, something is not right; something in the heart is not Christian....

May the Virgin Mary help us to walk along the path of love, love that is generous towards others, the way of the Good Samaritan. May she help us to live the first commandment that Christ left us. This is the way to enter into eternal life.

ANGELUS, ST. PETER'S SQUARE
SUNDAY, JULY 10, 2016

MIRROR OF THE TRINITY

The Feast of the Most Holy Trinity invites us to commit ourselves in daily events to being leaven of communion, consolation and mercy. In this mission, we are sustained by the strength that the Holy Spirit gives us: he takes care of the flesh of humanity, wounded by injustice, oppression, hate and avarice.

The Virgin Mary, in her humility, welcomed the Father's will and conceived the Son by the Holy Spirit. May she, Mirror of the Trinity, help us to strengthen our faith in the Trinitarian mystery and to translate it in to action with choices and attitudes of love and unity.

ANGELUS, ST. PETER'S SQUARE
SUNDAY, MAY 22, 2016, FEAST OF THE MOST HOLY TRINITY

BEAR WITNESS TO JESUS

Mary's gaze is not directed towards us alone. At the foot of the Cross, when Jesus entrusted to her the Apostle John, and with him all of us, in the words: "Woman, here is your son" (John 19:26), the gaze of Mary was fixed on Jesus. Mary says to us what she said at the wedding feast of Cana: "Do whatever he tells you" (John 2:5). Mary points to Jesus, she asks us to bear witness to Jesus, she constantly guides us to her Son, Jesus, because in him alone do we find salvation. He alone can change the water of our loneliness, difficulties and sin into the wine of encounter, joy and forgiveness. He alone.

VIDEO MESSAGE FOR PRAYER VIGIL AT THE SHRINE OF
DIVINE LOVE, FROM THE VATICAN
SATURDAY, OCTOBER 12, 2013

MODEL OF MEDITATION

May the Virgin Mary, model of meditation of the words and acts of the Lord, help us to rediscover with faith the beauty and richness of the Eucharist and of the other sacraments, which render present God's faithful love for us. In this way, we fall ever more in love with the Lord Jesus, our Bridegroom, and we go to meet him with our lamps alight with our joyous faith, thus becoming his witnesses in the world.

ANGELUS, ST. PETER'S SQUARE
SUNDAY, JANUARY 10, 2016

AN ICON OF FAITH

You have before you the example of Our Lady, to whom we pray with particular devotion in this month of May. Like her, never tire of "leaving," of going in haste to encounter and bring the presence of God (cf. Luke 1:39). She brings the presence of God because she is in profound communion with him. "Blessed is she who believed" (Luke 1:45), Elizabeth says to her. Mary is the icon of faith. Only in faith does one bear Jesus rather than oneself. In this Holy Year of Mercy, as we strive to follow the path of the works of mercy, we are called to renew ourselves in faith. In order to bring the Lord's presence to those who suffer in body and spirit, we must cultivate the faith, that faith that is born of listening to the Word of God and seeking profound communion with Jesus.

I encourage you to continue in your witness to the Gospel of charity, to be increasingly a sign and instrument of God's tenderness toward each person, especially the most fragile and cast aside.

ADDRESS TO MEMBERS OF ST PETER'S CIRCLE,
CLEMENTINE HALL
MONDAY, MAY 9, 2016

Pope Francis @Pontifex · May 4, 2013
Let us ask our Lady to teach us how to live out our faith in our daily lives and to make more room for the Lord.

OUR LADY'S PERSEVERANCE

Something…that Our Lady's Presentation makes me think of is perseverance. In the evocative iconography associated with this feast, the Child Mary is shown moving away from her parents as she climbs the steps of the Temple. Mary does not look back and, in a clear reference to the evangelical admonition, she moves forward with determination. We, like the disciples in the Gospel, also need to move forward as we bring to all peoples and places the Good News of Jesus.

ADDRESS TO CLERGY, RELIGIOUS AND SEMINARIANS,
QUITO, ECUADOR
WEDNESDAY, JULY 8, 2015

PRAY FOR A MERCIFUL HEART

Let us ask the Lord, each of us, for eyes that know how to see beyond appearance; ears that know how to listen to cries, whispers, and also silence; hands able to support, embrace and minister. Most of all let us ask for a great and merciful heart that desires the good and salvation of all. May Mary Immaculate and my blessing accompany you on your journey. And I thank you because I know you pray for me!

Our Lady always followed Jesus, to the end she accompanied him. Let us pray to her that she may always accompany us on our path: this path of joy, this path of going on: this journey of staying with Jesus.

ADDRESS TO THE ITALIAN CATHOLIC ACTION, PAUL VI
AUDIENCE HALL,
SATURDAY, MAY 3, 2014

WALK WITH THE HOLY SPIRIT

The Virgin Mary teaches us what it means to live in the Holy Spirit and what it means to accept the news of God in our life. She conceived Jesus by the work of the Holy Spirit, and every Christian, each one of us, is called to accept the Word of God, to accept Jesus inside of us and then to bring him to everyone. Mary invoked the Holy Spirit with the Apostles in the Upper Room: we too, every time that we come together in prayer, are sustained by the spiritual presence of the Mother of Jesus, in order to receive the gift of the Spirit and to have the strength to witness to Jesus Risen....

May Mary help you to be attentive to what the Lord asks of you, and to live and walk forever with the Holy Spirit!

REGINA COELI, ST. PETER'S SQUARE
SUNDAY, APRIL 28, 2013

IN OBEDIENCE TO THE WORD OF GOD

May the Lord Jesus Christ, the Incarnate Word of God and the divine Teacher who opened the minds and hearts of his disciples to understand the Scriptures (cf. Luke 24:45), always guide and support you in your activities. May the Virgin Mary, our model of docility and obedience to the Word of God, teach you to recognize fully the inexhaustible riches of Sacred Scripture, not only through intellectual research but also in prayer and in the whole of your life as believers, especially in this Year of Faith, so that your work may help make the light of Sacred Scripture shine in the hearts of the faithful.

ADDRESS TO THE PONTIFICAL BIBLICAL COMMISSION,
HALL OF POPES,
FRIDAY, APRIL 12, 2013

Pope Francis @Pontifex · December 8, 2014

Let us learn from the Virgin Mary how to be bolder in obeying the Word of God.

A MODEL OF TRUST IN GOD

Mary lived perpetually immersed in the mystery of God-made-man, as his first and perfect disciple, by contemplating all things in her heart in the light of the Holy Spirit, in order to understand and live out the will of God.

We can ask ourselves a question: Do we allow ourselves to be illumined by the faith of Mary, who is our Mother? Or do we think of her as distant, as someone too different from us? In moments of difficulty, of trial, of darkness, do we look to her as a model of trust in God who always and only desires our good? Let's think about this: perhaps it will do us good to rediscover Mary as the model and figure of the Church in this faith that she possessed!

GENERAL AUDIENCE, ST. PETER'S SQUARE
WEDNESDAY, OCTOBER 23, 2013

MARY, SHOW US THE WAY

Lord, you left your Mother in our midst that she might accompany us.

May she take care of us and protect us on our journey, in our hearts, in our faith.

May she make us disciples like herself, missionaries like herself.

May she teach us to go out onto the streets.

May she teach us to step outside ourselves....

May she, by her meekness, by her peace, show us the way.

PRAYER AFTER MEETING WITH YOUNG PEOPLE FROM
ARGENTINA, RIO DE JANEIRO
THURSDAY, JULY 25, 2013

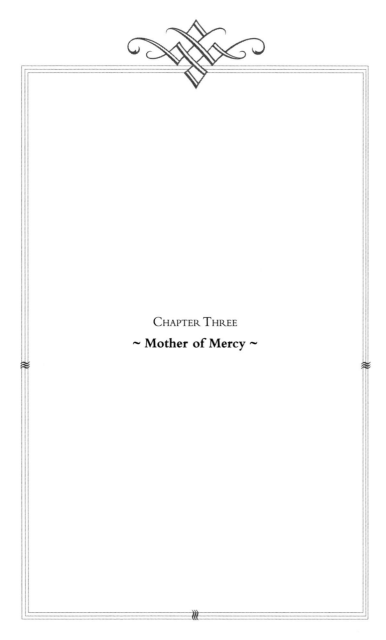

CHAPTER THREE

~ **Mother of Mercy** ~

MERCY MADE FLESH

My thoughts now turn to the Mother of Mercy.... No one has penetrated the profound mystery of the incarnation like Mary. Her entire life was patterned after the presence of mercy made flesh. The Mother of the Crucified and Risen One has entered the sanctuary of divine mercy because she participated intimately in the mystery of his love.

Chosen to be the Mother of the Son of God, Mary, from the outset, was prepared by the love of God to be the Ark of the Covenant between God and man. She treasured divine mercy in her heart in perfect harmony with her Son Jesus. Her hymn of praise, sung at the threshold of the home of Elizabeth, was dedicated to the mercy of God which extends from "generation to generation" (Luke 1:50). We too were included in those prophetic words of the Virgin Mary.

MISERICORDIAE VULTUS, (PAPAL BULL ON THE EXTRAORDINARY JUBILEE OF MERCY), 24 SATURDAY, APRIL 11, 2015

HAIL, MOTHER OF MERCY!

Salve, Mater Misericordiae!

With this invocation we turn to the Blessed Virgin Mary in the Roman Basilica dedicated to her under the title of Mother of God. It is the first line of an ancient hymn which we will sing at the conclusion of this Holy Eucharist. Composed by an unknown author, it has come down to us as a heartfelt prayer spontaneously rising up from the hearts of the faithful: "Hail Mother of mercy, Mother of God, Mother of forgiveness, Mother of hope, Mother of grace and Mother full of holy gladness." In these few words, we find a summary of the faith of generations of men and women who, with their eyes fixed firmly on the icon of the Blessed Virgin, have sought her intercession and consolation.

HOMILY, BASILICA OF ST. MARY MAJOR
FRIDAY, JANUARY 1, 2016, SOLEMNITY OF MARY,
MOTHER OF GOD

THE ADVENTURE OF MERCY

Whoever welcomes Jesus, learns to love as Jesus does. So he asks us if we want a full life. And in his name, I ask you: do you want a full life? Start right this moment by letting yourself be open and attentive! Because happiness is sown and blossoms in mercy. That is his answer, his offer, his challenge, his adventure: mercy. Mercy always has a youthful face...like that of Mary of Nazareth, whose daring "Yes" launched her on the adventure of mercy. All generations would call her blessed; to all of us she is the "Mother of Mercy." Let us call upon her together: Mary, Mother of Mercy. All of us: Mary, Mother of Mercy.

ADDRESS TO THE YOUNG PEOPLE OF
WORLD YOUTH DAY, KRAKOW (POLAND)
THURSDAY, JULY 28, 2016

VESSEL AND SOURCE OF MERCY

Ascending the stairway of the saints in our pursuit of vessels of mercy, we come at last to Our Lady. She is the simple yet perfect vessel that both receives and bestows mercy. Her free "yes" to grace is the very opposite of the sin that led to the downfall of the prodigal son. Her mercy is very much her own, very much our own and very much that of the Church. As she says in the Magnificat, she knows that God has looked with favor upon her humility and she recognizes that his mercy is from generation to generation. Mary can see the working of this mercy and she feels "embraced," together with all of Israel, by it. She treasures in her heart the memory and promise of God's infinite mercy for his people. Hers is the Magnificat of a pure and overflowing heart that sees all of history and each individual person with a mother's mercy.

SPIRITUAL RETREAT FOR PRIESTS,
BASILICA OF ST. MARY MAJOR, ROME
THURSDAY, JUNE 2, 2016

Pope Francis @Pontifex · May 31, 2016

I join spiritually all those taking part in special devotions to the Blessed Virgin Mary on this last day of the month of May.

MARY IS EVER AT OUR SIDE

It is most fitting that on this day we invoke the Blessed Virgin Mary above all as Mother of mercy. The door we have opened is, in fact, a door of Mercy. Those who cross its threshold are called to enter into the merciful love of the Father with complete trust and freedom from fear; they can leave this basilica knowing—truly knowing—that Mary is ever at their side. She is the Mother of mercy, because she bore in her womb the very face of divine mercy, Jesus, Emmanuel, the expectation of the nations, the "Prince of Peace" (Isaiah 9:5). The Son of God, made Incarnate for our salvation, has given us his Mother, who joins us on our pilgrimage through this life, so that we may never be left alone, especially at times of trouble and uncertainty.

HOMILY, BASILICA OF ST. MARY MAJOR
FRIDAY, JANUARY 1, 2016, SOLEMNITY OF MARY,
MOTHER OF GOD

A HEART FULL OF MERCY

The wedding feast of Cana is an image of the Church: at the center there is Jesus who in his mercy performs a sign; around him are the disciples, the first fruits of the new community; and beside Jesus and the disciples is Mary, the provident and prayerful Mother. Mary partakes of the joy of ordinary people and helps it to increase; she intercedes with her Son on behalf of the spouses and all the invited guests. Nor does Jesus refuse the request of his Mother. How much hope there is in that event for all of us! We have a Mother with benevolent and watchful eyes, like her Son; a heart that is maternal and full of mercy, like him; hands that want to help, like the hands of Jesus who broke bread for those who were hungry, touched the sick and healed them. All this fills us with trust and opens our hearts to the grace and mercy of Christ.

MESSAGE FOR THE WORLD DAY OF THE SICK 2016,
FROM THE VATICAN
TUESDAY, SEPTEMBER 15, 2015

LET OUR LADY GAZE AT YOU

We can conclude by praying the Salve Regina. The words of this prayer are vibrant with the mystery of the Magnificat. Mary is the Mother of mercy, our life, our sweetness and our hope. Whenever you priests have moments of darkness or distress, whenever your hearts are troubled, I would encourage you not only to "look to your Mother"—you should do that anyway—but to go to her, let her gaze at you, be still and even fall asleep in her presence. Your distress, and all those mistakes that may have brought it about…all that muck will become a vessel of mercy. Let Our Lady gaze at you!

Her eyes of mercy are surely the greatest vessel of mercy, for their gaze enables us to drink in that kindness and goodness for which we hunger with a yearning that only a look of love can satisfy. Mary's eyes of mercy also enable us to see God's mercy at work in human history and to find Jesus in the faces of our brothers and sisters. In Mary, we catch a glimpse of the promised land—the Kingdom of mercy established by the Lord—already present in this life beyond the exile into which sin leads us.

SPIRITUAL RETREAT FOR PRIESTS,
BASILICA OF ST. MARY MAJOR
THURSDAY, JUNE 2, 2016

Pope Francis @Pontifex · February 14, 2016
Simply looking at you, O Mother, to have eyes only for you, looking upon you without saying anything...

A PLACE OF REST AND HEALING

What people seek in the eyes of Mary is "a place of rest where people, still orphans and disinherited, may find a place of refuge, a home." And that has to do with the way she "gazes"—her eyes open up a space that is inviting, not at all like a tribunal or an office. If at times you realize that your own gaze has become hardened from hard work or weariness—this is something that happens to us all— or that you tend to look at people with annoyance or coldness, stop and look once again to her in heartfelt humility.

For Our Lady can remove every "cataract" that prevents you from seeing Christ in people's souls. She can remove the myopia that fails to see the needs of others, which are the needs of the Incarnate Lord, as well as the hyperopia that cannot see the details, "the small print," where the truly important things are played out in the life of the Church and of the family. Our Lady's gaze brings healing.

SPIRITUAL RETREAT FOR PRIESTS,
BASILICA OF ST. MARY MAJOR
THURSDAY, JUNE 2, 2016

GOD'S MERCY KNOWS NO BOUNDS

At the foot of the cross, Mary, together with John, the disciple of love, witnessed the words of forgiveness spoken by Jesus. This supreme expression of mercy towards those who crucified him shows us the point to which the mercy of God can reach. Mary attests that the mercy of the Son of God knows no bounds and extends to everyone, without exception. Let us address her in the words of the *Salve Regina*, a prayer ever ancient and ever new, so that she may never tire of turning her merciful eyes upon us, and make us worthy to contemplate the face of mercy, her Son Jesus.

MISERICORDIAE VULTUS, (PAPAL BULL ON THE
EXTRAORDINARY JUBILEE OF MERCY) 24
SATURDAY, APRIL 11, 2015

MOTHER OF FORGIVENESS

Mary is the Mother of God, she is the Mother of God who forgives, who bestows forgiveness, and so we can rightly call her Mother of forgiveness.

This word—"forgiveness"—so misunderstood in today's world, points to the new and original fruit of Christian faith. A person unable to forgive has not yet known the fullness of love. Only one who truly loves is able to forgive and forget. At the foot of the Cross, Mary sees her Son offer himself totally, showing us what it means to love as God loves. At that moment, she heard Jesus utter words which probably reflected what he had learned from her as a child: "Father, forgive them; for they do not know what they are doing" (Luke 23:24). At that moment, Mary became for all of us the Mother of forgiveness. Following Jesus's example and by his grace, she herself could forgive those who killed her innocent Son.

HOMILY, BASILICA OF ST. MARY MAJOR
FRIDAY, JANUARY 1, 2016, SOLEMNITY OF MARY,
MOTHER OF GOD

GOD'S MOTHER IS NEAR

"The Lord is near," the apostle Paul tells us, and nothing should perturb us. He is close by. He is not alone but is with his Mother. She said to St. Juan Diego: "Why are you afraid? Am I not here who am your Mother?" He is near. He and his Mother.

HOMILY, VATICAN BASILICA
SATURDAY, DECEMBER 12, 2015,
FEAST OF OUR LADY OF GUADALUPE

Pope Francis @Pontifex · December 10, 2013

Mary, Our Mother, sustain us in moments of darkness, difficulty and apparent defeat.

THE CHURCH TOO MUST FORGIVE

For us, Mary is an icon of how the Church must offer forgiveness to those who seek it. The Mother of forgiveness teaches the Church that the forgiveness granted on Golgotha knows no limits. Neither the law with its quibbles, nor the wisdom of this world with its distinctions, can hold it back. The Church's forgiveness must be every bit as broad as that offered by Jesus on the Cross and by Mary at his feet. There is no other way.

HOMILY, BASILICA OF ST. MARY MAJOR
FRIDAY, JANUARY 1, 2016, SOLEMNITY OF MARY,
MOTHER OF GOD

Pope Francis @Pontifex · May 27, 2016
Mary is an icon of how the Church must offer forgiveness to those who seek it.

A SIGN AND SACRAMENT OF MERCY

Holding Mary's hand and beneath her gaze, we can joyfully proclaim the greatness of the Lord. We can say: "My soul sings of you, Lord, for you have looked with favor on the lowliness and humility of your servant. How blessed I am, to have been forgiven. Your mercy, Lord, that you showed to your saints and to all your faithful people, you have also shown to me. I was lost, seeking only myself, in the arrogance of my heart, yet I found no glory. My only glory is that your Mother has embraced me, covered me with her mantle, and drawn me to her heart. I want to be loved as one of your little ones. I want to feed with your bread all those who hunger for you."

Remember, Lord, your covenant of mercy with your sons, the priests of your people. With Mary, may we be the sign and sacrament of your mercy.

SPIRITUAL RETREAT FOR PRIESTS,
BASILICA OF ST. MARY MAJOR
THURSDAY, JUNE 2, 2016

"I AM HERE TO HELP YOU"

This evening I am united to all of you in praying the Holy Rosary and in Eucharistic Adoration under the gaze of the Virgin Mary.

Mary's gaze! How important this is! How many things can we say with a look! Affection, encouragement, compassion, love, but also disapproval, envy, pride and even hatred. Often a look says more than words; it says what words do not or dare not say.

At whom is the Virgin Mary looking? She is looking at each and every one of us. And how does she look at us? She looks at us as a Mother, with tenderness, mercy and love. That was how she gazed at her Son Jesus at all the moments of his life—joyful, luminous, sorrowful, glorious—as we contemplate in the mysteries of the Holy Rosary, simply and lovingly.

When we are weary, downcast, beset with cares, let us look to Mary, let us feel her gaze, which speaks to our heart and says: "Courage, my child, I am here to help you!"

VIDEO MESSAGE FOR PRAYER VIGIL AT THE SHRINE OF DIVINE LOVE, FROM THE VATICAN
SATURDAY, OCTOBER 12, 2013

MARY, HELP US TRUST IN GOD'S MERCY

Nothing is impossible for God's mercy! Even the most tangled knots are loosened by his grace. And Mary, whose "yes" opened the door for God to undo the knot of the ancient disobedience, is the Mother who patiently and lovingly brings us to God, so that he can untangle the knots of our soul by his fatherly mercy. We all have some of these knots and we can ask in our heart of hearts: What are the knots in my life? "Father, my knots cannot be undone!" It is a mistake to say anything of the sort! All the knots of our heart, every knot of our conscience, can be undone. Do I ask Mary to help me trust in God's mercy, to undo those knots, to change? She, as a woman of faith, will surely tell you: "Get up, go to the Lord: he understands you." And she leads us by the hand as a Mother, our Mother, to the embrace of our Father, the Father of mercies.

PRAYER FOR MARIAN DAY, ST. PETER'S SQUARE
OCTOBER 12, 2013

A TRUE CHRISTIAN IS MERCIFUL

May the Blessed Virgin, first fruit of the saved, model of the Church, holy and immaculate spouse, loved by the Lord, help us to ever increasingly rediscover divine mercy as the distinguishing mark of Christians. One cannot understand a true Christian who is not merciful, just as one cannot comprehend God without his mercy. This is the epitomizing word of the Gospel: mercy. It is the fundamental feature of the face of Christ: that face that we recognize in the various aspects of his existence: when he goes to meet everyone, when he heals the sick, when he sits at the table with sinners, and above all when, nailed to the cross, he forgives; there we see the face of divine mercy.

ANGELUS, ST. PETER'S SQUARE
DECEMBER 8, 2015

IN TIMES OF PAIN

To all those who assist the sick and the suffering, I express my confident hope that they will draw inspiration from Mary, the Mother of mercy. "May the sweetness of her countenance watch over us in this Holy Year, so that all of us may rediscover the joy of God's tenderness" (papal bull *Misericordiae Vultus*, 24), allow it to dwell in our hearts and express it in our actions! Let us entrust to the Virgin Mary our trials and tribulations, together with our joys and consolations. Let us beg her to turn her eyes of mercy towards us, especially in times of pain, and make us worthy of beholding, today and always, the merciful face of her Son Jesus!

MESSAGE FOR THE WORLD DAY OF THE SICK 2016, FROM THE VATICAN
TUESDAY, SEPTEMBER 15, 2015

INTIMATELY UNITED TO JESUS

In Mary, God rejoices and is especially pleased. In one of the prayers dearest to Christians, the Salve Regina, we call Mary "Mother of Mercy." She has experienced divine mercy, and has hosted in her womb the very source of this mercy: Jesus Christ. She, who has always lived intimately united to her Son, knows better than anyone what he wants: that all men be saved, and that God's tenderness and consolation never fail anyone. May Mary, Mother of Mercy, help us to understand how much God loves us.

HOMILY, VATICAN BASILICA
SATURDAY, DECEMBER 12, 2015, FEAST OF OUR LADY OF
GUADALUPE

Pope Francis @Pontifex · February 12, 2016

In Mexico I will look into the eyes of the Virgin Mary and implore her to look upon us always with mercy. I entrust my journey to her.

CALLED TO BE WITNESSES OF MERCY

The night can seem vast and very dark, but in these days I have been able to observe that in this people there are many lights who proclaim hope; I have been able to see in many of their testimonies, in their faces, the presence of God who carries on walking in this land, guiding you, sustaining hope; many men and women, with their everyday efforts, make it possible for this Mexican society not to be left in darkness. Many men and women, lining the streets as I went by, lifted up their children, showing them to me: they are the future of Mexico, let us look after them, let us love them. These children are tomorrow's prophets; they are the sign of a new dawn. And I assure you that on some occasions, as I passed by, I felt I wanted to cry on seeing so much hope among people who suffer so much.

May Mary, Mother of Guadalupe, continue to visit you, continue to walk on your lands—Mexico which cannot be understood without her—may she continue helping you to be missionaries and witnesses of mercy and reconciliation.

FAREWELL AFTER MASS, CIUDAD JUÁREZ, MEXICO
WEDNESDAY, FEBRUARY 17, 2016

MAY WE GROW IN MERCY

In the end we will all be judged by the same measure with which we have judged: the mercy we have shown to others will also be shown to us. Let us ask Our Lady, our Mother, to help us to grow in patience, in hope and in mercy with all brothers and sisters.

ANGELUS, ST. PETER'S SQUARE
SUNDAY, JULY 20, 2014

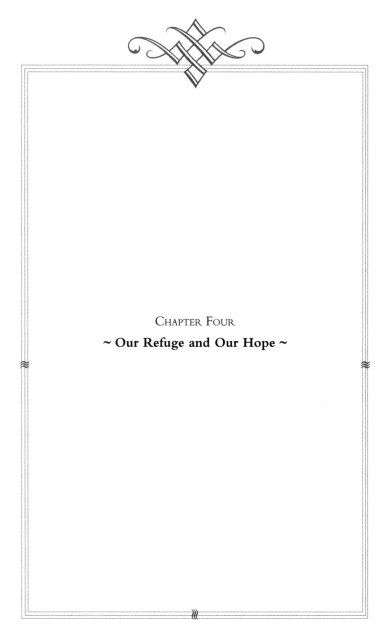

CHAPTER FOUR

~ Our Refuge and Our Hope ~

TURN TO MARY WITH CHILDLIKE TRUST

The Virgin Mary is always near us, as a caring mother. She is the first disciple of the Lord, the first example of a life dedicated to him and to his brothers. When we find ourselves in difficulty, or when faced with a situation that makes us feel the depth of our powerlessness, let us turn to her with childlike trust. Then she always says to us—as at the wedding at Cana—"Do whatever he tells you" (John 2:5). She teaches us to listen to Jesus and to follow his word, but to do so with faith! This is her secret, which as a mother, she wishes to transmit to us: faith, a genuine faith, enough so that even a grain of it can move mountains!

ADDRESS TO PRIESTS, MEN AND WOMEN RELIGIOUS,
AND SEMINARIANS GATHERED IN THE CATHEDRAL,
SARAJEVO, BOSNIA AND HERZEGOVINA
SATURDAY, JUNE 6, 2015

CLING TO OUR LADY'S MANTLE

Let Our Lady take you by the hand, and cling to her mantle. In my office, I have a lovely image of the *Synkatabasis* that Father Rupnik gave me. It shows Mary holding out her hands like a stairway on which Jesus descends. What I like most about it is that Jesus holds in one hand the fullness of the Law and with the other he clings to her mantle. In the Russian tradition, the old monks tell us that amid spiritual storms we need to take refuge under the mantle of Mary. The first Marian antiphon in the West says the same thing: *Sub Tuum Praesidium* [We fly to thy protection].

SPIRITUAL RETREAT FOR PRIESTS,
BASILICA OF ST. MARY MAJOR, ROME
THURSDAY, JUNE 2, 2016

OUR MOTHER IN HEAVEN

St. Leopold Mandi used to say that "the mercy of God exceeds our every expectation." He also used to say to someone suffering: "We have in heaven the heart of a mother. The Virgin, our Mother, who at the foot of the cross endured the most a human being can suffer, she understands our troubles and she consoles us." May Mary, refuge of sinners and Mother of mercy, ever guide and sustain the fundamental mystery of reconciliation.

ADDRESS TO PARTICIPANTS IN A COURSE SPONSORED
BY THE APOSTOLIC PENITENTIARY,
SALA REGIA,
FRIDAY, MARCH 2, 2016

MARY IS READY TO COME TO OUR AID

Today, at the end of the month of Mary, is the feast on which we remember her visit to St. Elizabeth. The Gospel (of Luke) tells us that, after the annunciation of the angel, she went in haste, she lost no time, she went immediately out to serve. She is the Virgin *of readiness*, Our Lady of readiness. She is ready right away to come to our aid when we pray to her, when we ask for her help; her protection is in our favor. In many of life's moments when we stand in need of her help, her protection, let us remember that she does not make us wait: she is Our Lady of readiness, she immediately goes to serve.

WORDS AFTER RECITATION OF THE HOLY ROSARY,
GARDENS OF VATICAN CITY
SATURDAY, MAY 31, 2014

Pope Francis @Pontifex · August 13, 2015
Mary is full of grace. She is a sure refuge for us in times of temptation.

REFUGE OF SINNERS

Let us entrust ourselves to the intercession of Mary, Mother of mercy and refuge of sinners. She knows how to help us, we sinners. I really like reading the stories of St. Alphonsus Maria de Liguori, and various chapters of his book, *The Glories of Mary*. These stories of Our Lady, who is ever the refuge of sinners and seeks the way for the Lord to forgive all. May she teach us this art. I heartily bless you. I ask you to please pray for me. Thank you.

ADDRESS TO PARTICIPANTS IN A COURSE ORGANIZED
BY THE APOSTOLIC PENITENTIARY,
CLEMENTINE HALL,
THURSDAY, MARCH 12, 2015

DELIVER US FROM ALL DANGERS

To Mary, Mother of God and our Mother, let us present our good intentions. We ask you to extend the mantle of your maternal protection over each and every one of us in the new year: "O Holy Mother of God despise not our petitions in our necessities, but deliver us always from all dangers, O glorious and blessed Virgin" (*Sub tuum praesidium*).

And I invite you all to greet Our Lady as the Mother of God, hail her with this salute: "Holy Mother of God!" As she was acclaimed, at the start of Christianity, when at the entrance of the Church they would cry out to their pastors this salute to Our Lady: "Holy Mother of God!" All together, three times, let us repeat: "Holy Mother of God."

ANGELUS, ST. PETER'S SQUARE,
THURSDAY, JANUARY 1, 2015, SOLEMNITY OF MARY,
MOTHER OF GOD

TRUST IN OUR LADY'S ASSISTANCE

We are gathered here in front of the Shrine of Our Lady of Sorrows, built in 1888 in the place where two girls from this area, Fabiana and Serafina, had a vision of the Mother of God while they were working in the fields. Mary is Mother, she always assists us: when we are working and when we are looking for work, when we have clear ideas and when we are confused, when prayer flows spontaneously and when the heart is desolate: She is always there to help us. Mary is the Mother of God, our Mother and Mother of the Church. So many men and women, young and old have turned to her to say "thank you" and to beg a favor. Mary takes us to Jesus and Jesus gives us peace. Let us turn to her, trusting in her assistance, with courage and hope.

ADDRESS TO YOUNG PEOPLE OF THE DIOCESES OF
ABRUZZI AND MOLISE, ITALY
SATURDAY, JULY 5, 2014

YOU ARE IN GOOD HANDS

You are fortunate because you are in good hands! They are motherly hands that always protect, that are open in order to welcome....

Mary is the one who, with prayer and love, in silent action, transformed the Sabbath of disappointment into the dawn of the Resurrection. If some feel weary and oppressed by the circumstances of life, let them trust in our Mother who is close to us and consoles, because she is Mother! She always heartens us and invites us to again put trust in God: his Son will not betray our expectations and will sow in our hearts a hope that does not disappoint.

ADDRESS, MEETING WITH THE WORLD OF LABOR,
PRATO, ITALY
TUESDAY, NOVEMBER 10, 2015

MARY'S TENDERNESS

In Mary's concern, we see reflected the tenderness of God. This same tenderness is present in the lives of all those persons who attend the sick and understand their needs, even the most imperceptible ones, because they look upon them with eyes full of love. How many times has a mother at the bedside of her sick child, or a child caring for an elderly parent, or a grandchild concerned for a grandparent, placed his or her prayer in the hands of Our Lady!

MESSAGE FOR THE WORLD DAY OF THE SICK,
FROM THE VATICAN
TUESDAY, SEPTEMBER 15, 2015

OUR LADY IS NEAR TO US

After concluding the dialogue with the apostles, Jesus addressed everyone, saying: "If anyone wants to come after me, let him deny himself, take up his cross daily and follow me" (Luke 9:23). This is not an ornamental cross or an ideological cross, but it is the cross of life, the cross of one's duty, the cross of making sacrifices for others with love—for parents, for children, for the family, for friends, and even for enemies—the cross of being ready to be in solidarity with the poor, to strive for justice and peace.... On this path, Our Lady is always near to us: let us allow her to hold our hand when we are going through the darkest and most difficult moments.

ANGELUS, ST. PETER'S SQUARE
SUNDAY, JUNE 19, 2016

Pope Francis @Pontifex · April 17, 2015
Mary, Mother of sorrows, help us to understand God's will in moments of great suffering.

AM I NOT YOUR MOTHER?

Visiting this shrine, the same things that happened to Juan Diego can also happen to us. Look at the Blessed Mother from within our own sufferings, our own fear, hopelessness, sadness, and say to her, "What can I offer since I am not learned?" We look to our Mother with eyes that express our thoughts: there are so many situations which leave us powerless, which make us feel that there is no room for hope, for change, for transformation....

And in the silence, and in this looking at her, we will hear what she says to us once more, "What, my most precious little one, saddens your heart?" (*Nican Mopohua*, 107) "Yet am I not here with you, who have the honor of being your Mother?" (*Nican Mopohua*, 119).

Mary tells us that she has "the honor" of being our Mother, assuring us that those who suffer do not weep in vain. These ones are a silent prayer rising to heaven, always finding a place in Mary's mantle. In her and with her, God has made himself our Brother and companion along the journey; he carries our crosses with us so as not to leave us overwhelmed by our sufferings.

Am I not your Mother? Am I not here? Do not let trials and pains overwhelm you, she tells us.

HOMILY, BASILICA OF OUR LADY OF GUADALUPE,
MEXICO CITY
SATURDAY, FEBRUARY 12, 2016

Pope Francis @Pontifex · December 12, 2014
Our Lady of Guadalupe, pray for us!

MARY WIPES AWAY OUR TEARS

At the foot of every cross, the Mother of Jesus is always there. With her mantle, she wipes away our tears. With her outstretched hand, she helps us to rise up and she accompanies us along the path of hope.

PRAYER VIGIL TO "DRY THE TEARS," VATICAN BASILICA, THURSDAY, MAY 5, 2016

Pope Francis @Pontifex · October 11, 2013

When we encounter the cross, we turn to Mary: Give us the strength, Mary our Mother, to accept and embrace the cross!"

WISDOM OF HEART

Even when illness, loneliness and inability make it hard for us to reach out to others, the experience of suffering can become a privileged means of transmitting grace and a source for gaining and growing in *sapientia cordis* [wisdom of the heart]. We come to understand how Job, at the end of his experience, could say to God: "I had heard of you by the hearing of the ear, but now my eye sees you" (Job 42:5). People immersed in the mystery of suffering and pain, when they accept these in faith, can themselves become living witnesses of a faith capable of embracing suffering, even without being able to understand its full meaning.

I entrust this World Day of the Sick to the maternal protection of Mary, who conceived and gave birth to wisdom incarnate: Jesus Christ, our Lord.

O Mary, seat of wisdom, intercede as our Mother for all the sick and for those who care for them! Grant that, through our service of our suffering neighbors, and through the experience of suffering itself, we may receive and cultivate true wisdom of heart!

MESSAGE FOR THE WORLD DAY OF THE SICK,
FROM THE VATICAN
WEDNESDAY, DECEMBER 3, 2014

WE ARE NOT ALONE

So many of you have lost everything. I do not know what to tell you. But surely he knows what to tell you! So many of you have lost members of your family. I can only be silent; I accompany you silently, with my heart....

Many of you looked to Christ and asked: Why, Lord? To each of you, the Lord responds from his heart. I have no other words to say to you. Let us look to Christ: he is the Lord, and he understands us, for he experienced all the troubles we experience.

With him, beneath the cross, is his Mother. We are like that child who stands down there, who, in times of sorrow and pain, times when we understand nothing, times when we want to rebel, can only reach out and cling to her skirts and say to her: "Mother!" Like a little child who is frightened and says: "Mother." Perhaps that is the only word which can express all the feelings we have in those dark moments: Mother!

Let us be still for a moment and look to the Lord. He can understand us, for he experienced all these things. And let us look to our Mother, and like that little child, let us reach out, cling to her skirts and say to her in our hearts: "Mother." Let us make this prayer in silence; let everyone say it whatever way he or she feels....

We are not alone; we have a Mother; we have Jesus, our older brother. We are not alone. And we also have many brothers and sisters who, when the disaster struck, came to our assistance. We too feel more like brothers and sisters whenever we help one another, whenever we help each other.

This is all that I feel I have to say to you. Forgive me if I have no other words. But be sure that Jesus does not disappoint us; be sure that the love and tenderness of our Mother does not disappoint us. Clinging to her as sons and daughters with the strength which Jesus our brother gives us, let us now move forward. As brothers and sisters, let us take up our journey. Thank you!

Dear brothers and sisters, throughout this ordeal you have felt the grace of God in a special way through the presence and loving care of the Blessed Virgin Mary, Our Lady of Perpetual Help. She is our Mother. May she help you to persevere in faith and hope, and to reach out to all in need.

HOMILY, TACLOBAN CITY INTERNATIONAL AIRPORT,
PHILIPPINES
SATURDAY, JANUARY 17, 2015

Pope Francis @Pontifex · February 24, 2014
Our Lady is always close to us, especially when we feel the weight of life with all its problems.

THE VIRGIN OF TEPEYAC

Tomorrow is the feast of Our Lady of Guadalupe, the patroness of the Americas. I would like to greet all my brothers and sisters on that continent, and I do so thinking of the Virgin of Tepeyac.

When Our Lady appeared to St. Juan Diego, her face was that of a woman of mixed blood, a *mestiza*, and her garments bore many symbols of the native culture. Like Jesus, Mary is close to all her sons and daughters; as a concerned mother, she accompanies them on their way through life. She shares all the joys and hopes, the sorrows and troubles of God's people, which is made up of men and women of every race and nation.

When the image of the Virgin appeared on the tilma of Juan Diego, it was the prophecy of an embrace: Mary's embrace of all the peoples of the vast expanses of America—the peoples who already lived there, and those who were yet to come. Mary's embrace showed what America—North and South—is called to be: a land where different peoples come together; a land prepared to accept human life at every stage, from the mother's womb to old age; a land which welcomes immigrants, and the poor and the marginalized, in every age. A land of generosity.

That is the message of Our Lady of Guadalupe, and it is also my message, the message of the Church. I ask all the people of the Americas to open wide their arms, like the Virgin, with love and tenderness.

MESSAGE TO THE AMERICAS FOR THE FEAST OF OUR
LADY OF GUADALUPE
GENERAL AUDIENCE, ST. PETER'S SQUARE
WEDNESDAY, DECEMBER 11, 2013

MAY OUR LADY LEAD US TO JESUS

I thank you and I would like to take advantage of this meeting with you, who work in the prisons throughout Italy, to send my greetings to all the inmates. Please tell them that I am praying for them, I have them at heart, I am praying to the Lord and to Our Lady that they may be able to get through this difficult period in their lives in a positive way, that they may not become discouraged or closed in on themselves....

It is my sincere wish that the Lord be always with you, that he bless you and that Our Lady watch over you; let yourselves remain always in the hands of Our Lady, for she is the mother of you and of all those in prison. This is my wish for you, thank you! And let us ask the Lord to bless you and all of your friends in the prisons; but let us first pray to Our Lady that she may always lead us to Jesus: Hail Mary...

ADDRESS TO PARTICIPANTS IN THE NATIONAL MEETING OF PRISON CHAPLAINS, AULA, PAUL VI AUDIENCE HALL, WEDNESDAY, OCTOBER 23, 2013

MARY GIVES US STRENGTH

Let us remember the parable of the good Samaritan: Jesus does not approve of the behavior of the priest or the Levite, who both avoid helping the man who was attacked by robbers, but the Samaritan who sees that man's state and confronts it in a concrete way, despite the risks. Mary saw many difficult moments in her life, from the birth of Jesus, when "there was no place for them in the inn" (Luke 2:7), to Calvary (cf. John 19:25). And like a good Mother she is close to us, so that we may never lose courage before the adversities of life, before our weakness, before our sins: she gives us strength, she shows us the path of her Son.

Jesus from the cross says to Mary, indicating John: "Woman, behold your son!" and to John: "Here is your mother!" (cf. John 19:26–27). In that disciple, we are all represented: the Lord entrusts us to the loving and tender hands of the Mother, that we might feel her support in facing and overcoming the difficulties of our human and Christian journey; to never be afraid of the struggle, to face it with the help of the mother.

ADDRESS AFTER RECITAL OF THE HOLY ROSARY,
BASILICA OF ST. MARY MAJOR
SATURDAY, MAY 4, 2013

PRAY FOR US SINNERS

Imitate Mary's motherhood, the maternal care that she has for each one of us. During the miracle at the wedding in Cana, our Lady turned to the servants and said to them: "Do whatever he tells you...." Mary's intercession with her Son shows the care of the Mother for people. It is a care which is attentive to our most concrete needs: Mary knows what we need! She takes care of us, interceding with Jesus and asking the gift of "new wine" for each one of us, i.e., the gift of love, of grace which saves us. She is always interceding and praying for us, especially at the hour of difficulty and weakness, at the hour of distress and confusion, and especially at the hour of sin. That is why, in the prayer of the Hail Mary, we ask her: "Pray for us sinners."

ADDRESS TO THE MEMBERS OF UNITALSI, PAUL VI
AUDIENCE HALL
SATURDAY, NOVEMBER 9, 2013

Pope Francis @Pontifex · August 15, 2013

Mary, Mother of God, pray for us sinners, and guide us on the way that leads to heaven.

DO WHATEVER OUR LADY TELLS YOU

I remember once at the shrine of Luján I was in the confessional, where there was a long queue. There was even a very modern young man, with earrings, tattoos, all these things.... And he came to tell me what was happening to him. It was a big and difficult problem. And he said to me: "I told my mother all this and my mother said to me, go to Our Lady and she will tell you what you must do." Here is a woman who had the gift of counsel. She did not know how to help her son out of his problem, but she indicated the right road: go to Our Lady and she will tell you. This is the gift of counsel. That humble, simple woman, gave her son the truest counsel. In fact, this young man said to me: "I looked at Our Lady and I felt that I had to do this, this and this...." I did not have to speak, his mother and the boy himself had already said everything.

GENERAL AUDIENCE, ST. PETER'S SQUARE
WEDNESDAY, MAY 7, 2014

WE FLY TO YOUR PROTECTION,
O HOLY MOTHER

The first piece of advice, when your heart is in turmoil, is the advice of the Russian fathers: go beneath the mantle of the Holy Mother of God. Remember that the first Latin antiphon is exactly this: in times of turmoil, take refuge under the mantle of the Holy Mother of God. It is the antiphon "*Sub tuum presidium confugimus, Sancta Dei Genitrix*" [We fly to your protection, O Holy Mother of God]. It is the first Latin antiphon dedicated to Our Lady. It's interesting, no?

Be watchful. Is there turmoil? First go there, and wait there until there is a bit of calm: through prayer, through entrustment to Our Lady.... One of you might say to me: "But father, in this time of such good modern advancements, of psychology, of psychiatry, in such moments of turmoil I think it would be better to go to a psychiatrist to help me...." I don't rule this out, but first go to your Mother, because a priest who forgets his Mother, especially in moments of turmoil, he's missing something.

He is an orphan priest: he has forgotten his Mother! And it's in the difficult moments that a child always goes to his mother. And we are children in the spiritual life. Never forget this! To be watchful over the state of my heart. In times of turmoil, go to seek refuge under the mantle of the Holy Mother of God. So say the Russian monks and, in truth, so it is.

ADDRESS TO RECTORS AND STUDENTS OF THE
PONTIFICAL COLLEGES AND RESIDENCES OF ROME,
PAUL VI AUDIENCE HALL
MONDAY, MAY 12, 2014

Pope Francis @Pontifex · August 15, 2016

I entrust you to the maternal care of our Mother who lives in the glory of God and is always by our side on our life's journey.

COURAGE, MY CHILD!

When we are weary, downcast, beset with cares, let us look to Mary, let us feel her gaze, which speaks to our heart and says: "Courage, my child, I am here to help you!" Our Lady knows us well, she is a Mother, she is familiar with our joys and difficulties, our hopes and disappointments. When we feel the burden of our failings and our sins, let us look to Mary, who speaks to our hearts, saying: "Arise, go to my Son Jesus; in him you will find acceptance, mercy and new strength for the journey."

VIDEO MESSAGE FOR PRAYER VIGIL AT THE SHRINE OF
DIVINE LOVE, FROM THE VATICAN
SATURDAY, OCTOBER 12, 2013

DELIVER US ALWAYS FROM ALL DANGERS

To Mary, Mother of God and our Mother, let us present our good intentions. We ask you to extend the mantle of your maternal protection over each and every one of us in the new year: "O Holy Mother of God despise not our petitions in our necessities, but deliver us always from all dangers, O glorious and blessed Virgin" (*Sub tuum praesidium*).

And I invite you all to greet Our Lady as the Mother of God, hail her with this salute: "Holy Mother of God!" As she was acclaimed, at the start of Christianity, when at the entrance of the Church they would cry out to their pastors this salute to Our Lady: "Holy Mother of God!" All together, three times, let us repeat: "Holy Mother of God."

ANGELUS, ST. PETER'S SQUARE
THURSDAY, JANUARY 1, 2015, SOLEMNITY OF MARY,
MOTHER OF GOD

CHAPTER FIVE

~ Star of the New Evangelization ~

MARIAN-STYLE MISSIONARIES

There is a Marian "style" to the Church's work of evangelization. Whenever we look to Mary, we come to believe once again in the revolutionary nature of love and tenderness. In her, we see that humility and tenderness are not virtues of the weak, but of the strong who need not treat others poorly in order to feel important themselves.

Contemplating Mary, we realize that she who praised God for "bringing down the mighty from their thrones" and "sending the rich away empty" (Luke 1:52–53) is also the one who brings a homely warmth to our pursuit of justice. She is also the one who carefully keeps "all these things, pondering them in her heart" (Luke 2:19). Mary is able to recognize the traces of God's Spirit in events great and small. She constantly contemplates the mystery of God in our world, in human history and in our daily lives. She is the woman of prayer and work in Nazareth, and she is also Our Lady of Help, who sets out from her town "with haste" (Luke 1:39) to be of service to others.

This interplay of justice and tenderness, of contemplation

and concern for others, is what makes the ecclesial community look to Mary as a model of evangelization. We implore her maternal intercession that the Church may become a home for many peoples, a Mother for all peoples, and that the way may be opened to the birth of a new world. It is the Risen Christ who tells us, with a power that fills us with confidence and unshakeable hope: "Behold, I make all things new" (Revelation 21:5).

APOSTOLIC EXHORTATION *EVANGELII GAUDIUM,* 288
NOVEMBER 24, 2013

Pope Francis @Pontifex · February 2, 2016
Mary, Mother of Jesus, help us to share the wonders of the Lord with all whom we meet on the way.

BE MY AMBASSADOR

Today, [Mary] sends us out anew; as she did Juancito. Today, she comes to tell us again: be my ambassador, the one I send to build many new shrines, accompany many lives, wipe away many tears. Simply be my ambassador by walking along the paths of your neighborhood, of your community, of your parish; we can build shrines by sharing the joy of knowing that we are not alone, that Mary accompanies us. Be my ambassador, she says to us, giving food to the hungry, drink to those who thirst, a refuge to those in need, clothe the naked and visit the sick. Come to the aid of those in prison, do not leave them alone, forgive whomever has offended you, console the grieving, be patient with others, and above all beseech and pray to God. And in the silence tell him what is in your heart.

HOMILY, BASILICA OF OUR LADY OF GUADALUPE,
MEXICO CITY
SATURDAY, FEBRUARY 13, 2016

GO OUT TO THE ENDS OF THE EARTH

Humanity is in such need of the Gospel, the source of joy, hope and peace. The mission to evangelize takes priority, for missionary activity is still today the Church's greatest challenge....

May the Virgin Mary, star of evangelization, obtain for us always a passion for the kingdom of God, so that the joy of the Gospel may reach the ends of the earth, and no periphery be deprived of its light.

ADDRESS, PONTIFICAL MISSION SOCIETIES,
CLEMENTINE HALL,
FRIDAY, JUNE 5, 2015

THE SPIRIT OF THE NEW EVANGELIZATION

With the Holy Spirit, Mary is always present in the midst of the people. She joined the disciples in praying for the coming of the Holy Spirit (Acts 1:14) and thus made possible the missionary outburst which took place at Pentecost. She is the Mother of the Church which evangelizes, and without her we could never truly understand the spirit of the new evangelization.

APOSTOLIC EXHORTATION *EVANGELII GAUDIUM*, 284
NOVEMBER 24, 2013

BEAR WITNESS TO MERCY

May the Virgin Mary, Mother of evangelizers, help us to strongly perceive the hunger and thirst for the Gospel that there is in the world, especially in the hearts and the flesh of the poor. May she enable each of us and every Christian community to tangibly bear witness to the mercy, the great mercy that Christ has given us.

ANGELUS, ST. PETER'S SQUARE,
SUNDAY, JANUARY 24, 2016

WITH OUR LADY'S GAZE

Let us look upon one another in a more fraternal way! Mary teaches us to have that gaze which strives to welcome, to accompany and to protect. Let us learn to look at one another beneath Mary's maternal gaze! There are people whom we instinctively consider less and who instead are in greater need: the most abandoned, the sick, those who have nothing to live on, those who do not know Jesus, youth who find themselves in difficulty, young people who cannot find work. Let us not be afraid to go out and to look upon our brothers and sisters with Our Lady's gaze. She invites us to be true brothers and sisters.

HOMILY, SHRINE OF OUR LADY OF BONARIA,
CAGLIARI, ITALY
SUNDAY, SEPTEMBER 22, 2013

BRING CHRIST TO OTHERS

We need to bring Christ to others...like Mary, who brought Christ to the hearts of men and women; we need to pass through the clouds of indifference without losing our way; we need to descend into the darkest night without being overcome and disorientated; we need to listen to the dreams, without being seduced; we need to share their disappointments, without becoming despondent; to sympathize with those whose lives are falling apart, without losing our own strength and identity. This is the path. This is the challenge.

ADDRESS, PONTIFICAL COUNCIL FOR SOCIAL
COMMUNICATIONS
SATURDAY, SEPTEMBER 21, 2013

Pope Francis @Pontifex · January 23, 2014

Like Mary, may we nurture the light born within us at Christmas. May we carry it everywhere in our daily lives.

THE EVANGELIZATION OF A CONTINENT

The spiritual "center of gravity" of my pilgrimage [to Mexico] was the shrine of Our Lady of Guadalupe. To remain in silence before the image of the Mother was my principal aim. I thank God that he gave me this opportunity. I contemplated and I allowed myself to be gazed upon by she who carries imprinted in her eyes the gaze of all her children, gathering up the sorrows caused by violence, kidnapping, assassinations, the violence against so many poor people, against so many women.

Guadalupe is the most visited Marian shrine in the world. From all over the Americas, people go to pray where *la Virgen Morenita* appeared to the Indian, St. Juan Diego, which set in motion the evangelization of the continent and its new civilization, a fruit of the encounter between diverse cultures.

ANGELUS, ST. PETER'S SQUARE
SUNDAY, FEBRUARY 21, 2016

ARE WE FAITHFUL TO CHRIST'S PLAN?

Let us ask ourselves: today, in our parish communities, in our associations, in our movements, are we faithful to Christ's plan? Is the priority evangelizing the poor, bringing them the joyful Good News? Pay heed: it does not only involve doing social assistance, much less political activity. It involves offering the strength of the Gospel of God, who converts hearts, heals wounds, and transforms human and social relationships according to the logic of love. The poor are indeed at the center of the Gospel.

May the Virgin Mary, Mother of evangelizers, help us to strongly perceive the hunger and thirst for the Gospel that there is in the world, especially in the hearts and the flesh of the poor. May she enable each of us and every Christian community to tangibly bear witness to the mercy, the great mercy that Christ has given us.

ANGELUS, ST. PETER'S SQUARE
SUNDAY, JANUARY 24, 2016

Pope Francis @Pontifex · August 14, 2014

Mary, Queen of Heaven, help us to transform the world according to God's plan.

A WORTHY AMBASSADOR

Mary, the woman who gave her "yes," wished also to come to the inhabitants of these American lands through the person of the Indian St. Juan Diego. Just as she went along the paths of Judea and Galilee, in the same way she walked through Tepeyac, wearing the indigenous garb and using their language so as to serve this great nation. Just as she accompanied Elizabeth in her pregnancy, so too she has and continues to accompany the development of this blessed Mexican land. Just as she made herself present to little Juan, so too she continues to reveal herself to all of us, especially to those who feel, like him, "worthless."

This specific choice, we might call it preferential, was not against anyone but rather in favor of everyone. The little Indian Juan who called himself a "leather strap, a back frame, a tail, a wing, oppressed by another's burden," became "the ambassador, most worthy of trust" (cf. *Nican Mopohua*, 55).

HOMILY, BASILICA OF OUR LADY OF GUADALUPE,
MEXICO CITY
SATURDAY, FEBRUARY 13, 2016

BE READY TO GO AND HELP

Mary sets out after hearing the word of the angel: "Your relative Elizabeth in her old age has also conceived a son…" (Luke 1:36).

Mary knows how to listen to God. It is not simply about hearing, but about listening attentively and receptively, and being ready to help. Think of how many times we come before the Lord or other people, but fail to really listen. Mary also listens to events, to things that happen in life. She is attentive to practical realities; she does not stop at the surface, but seeks to grasp their meaning. Mary knew that Elizabeth, now elderly, was expecting a child. She saw in this the hand of God, a sign of his mercy. The same thing also happens in our own lives. The Lord stands at the door and knocks in any number of ways; he posts signs along our path and he calls us to read them in the light of the Gospel.

ADDRESS TO WORLD YOUTH DAY VOLUNTEERS,
ORGANIZING COMMITTEE AND BENEFACTORS, KRAKOW,
POLAND
SUNDAY, JULY 31, 2016

A HERALD OF JOY

The image of Our Lady's Presentation tells us that, after being blessed by the priests, the child Mary began to dance at the foot of the altar. I think of the joy expressed in the imagery of the wedding feast, of the friend of the bridegroom, of the bride bedecked with her jewels. It is the happiness of all those who have discovered a treasure and left everything behind in order to gain it.

To find the Lord, to dwell in his house, to share in his life, commits us to proclaiming his kingdom and bringing his salvation to all. Crossing the threshold of the temple means becoming, like Mary, temples of the Lord and setting out to bring the good news to our brothers and sisters. Our Lady, as the first missionary disciple, once she had received the message of the angel, left with haste to a town of Judah to share this incredible joy, which led St. John the Baptist to leap in his mother's womb. The one who hears the Lord's voice "leaps with joy" and becomes for his or her own time a herald of his joy. The joy of evangelization leads the Church to go forth, like Mary.

ADDRESS TO CLERGY, RELIGIOUS AND SEMINARIANS,
QUITO, ECUADOR
WEDNESDAY, JULY 8, 2015

Pope Francis @Pontifex · September 13, 2013
Jesus is the sun and Mary is the dawn announcing his rising.

APOSTLES OF THE GOSPEL

To the young people and to all of you today I repeat: solve problems with solidarity. I therefore encourage you to be witnesses to solidarity in your cities and towns, at work, at school, in the family and at meeting places.

May the Virgin Mary make you attentive to the Word of God, may she transform you into humble, credible and effective apostles of the Gospel.

ADDRESS TO PILGRIMS FROM THE DIOCESE OF
ISERNIA-VENAFRO, PAUL VI AUDIENCE HALL,
SATURDAY, MAY 2, 2015

PROCLAIM THE GOOD NEWS

By becoming joyful proclaimers of the Gospel to their fellow citizens, the lay faithful discover that there are many hearts that the Holy Spirit has already prepared to receive their witness, their closeness and their attention....

I entrust your work and your projects to the maternal protection of the Virgin Mary, a pilgrim together with her Son in proclaiming the Gospel, from village to village, from city to city.

ADDRESS, PONTIFICAL COUNCIL FOR THE LAITY,
CLEMENTINE HALL
SATURDAY, FEBRUARY 7, 2015

MOTHER OF THE AMERICAS

The peoples and nations of our great Latin American homeland, with gratitude and joy, commemorate the feast of their patroness, Our Lady of Guadalupe, whose devotion spans from Alaska to Patagonia....

So many jumped for joy and hope at her visit and at the gift of her Son, and the perfect disciple of the Lord became the "great missionary who brought the Gospel to our Americas" (cf. *Aparecida Document*, n. 269)....

Through her intercession, the Christian faith began to grow into the most precious treasure of the soul of the American peoples, whose pearl of great value is Jesus Christ: a patrimony that has been passed on and is manifest still today in the baptism of multitudes of people, in the faith, in hope and charity of many, in the preciousness of popular piety and also in the American ethos which is shown in the awareness of human dignity, in the passion for justice, in solidarity with the poorest and the suffering, in the hope, at times, against all hope.

HOMILY, VATICAN BASILICA,
FRIDAY, DECEMBER 12, 2014,
FEAST OF OUR LADY OF GUADALUPE

A MISSIONARY HEART

Dear brothers and sisters, you have already borne much fruit for the Church and the world. You will bear even greater fruit with the help of the Holy Spirit, who raises up and renews his gifts and charisms, and through the intercession of Mary, who never ceases to assist and accompany her children. Go forward, always in movement...never stop but always keep moving! I assure you of my prayers and I ask you to pray for me—I have great need, truly—and I cordially impart to each of you my blessing.

I now ask you, together, to pray to Our Lady who had the experience of keeping alive the freshness of the first encounter with God, of moving forward in humility, always being on the way, respecting each person's time. She never tired of having this missionary heart.

ADDRESS, WORLD CONGRESS OF ECCLESIAL MOVEMENTS
AND NEW COMMUNITIES
SATURDAY, NOVEMBER 22, 2014

THE LESSON OF APARECIDA

The Church needs constantly to relearn the lesson of Aparecida; she must not lose sight of it. The Church's nets are weak, perhaps patched; the Church's barque is not as powerful as the great transatlantic liners which cross the ocean. And yet God wants to be seen precisely through our resources, scanty resources, because he is always the one who acts....

At times we lose people because they don't understand what we are saying, because we have forgotten the language of simplicity and import an intellectualism foreign to our people. Without the grammar of simplicity, the Church loses the very conditions which make it possible "to fish" for God in the deep waters of his mystery....

May the Virgin of Aparecida be the star which illumines your task and your journey of bringing Christ, as she did, to all the men and women of your immense country. Just as he did for the two lost and disillusioned disciples of Emmaus, he will warm your hearts and give you new and certain hope.

ADDRESS TO THE BISHOPS OF BRAZIL, RIO DE JANIERO
SATURDAY, JULY 28, 2013

LEAD US TO JESUS

Let us implore the Most Holy Virgin Mary, as Our Lady of Guadalupe—Mother of God, the queen and my lady, "my maiden, my little one," as St. Juan Diego called her, and with all the loving names by which we turn to her in popular piety—let us pray that she continue to accompany, help and protect our peoples. And may she lead by the hand all the children who go on pilgrimage to those lands to meet her Son, Jesus Christ, Our Lord, present in the Church, in his sacramental nature, especially in the Eucharist, present in the treasure of his Word and in his teaching, present in the holy and faithful people of God, present in those who are suffering and in the lowly in heart. And should we be frightened by such a bold plan or should worldly pusillanimity threaten us, may she return to speak to our heart and enable us to hear her voice, that of Mother, of "Good Mother," of "Great Mother": "Why are you afraid? Am I not here, I, who am your Mother?"

HOMILY, VATICAN BASILICA
FRIDAY, DECEMBER 12, 2014,
FEAST OF OUR LADY OF GUADALUPE

BE CONTEMPLATIVES AND MISSIONARIES

I would like a more missionary Church, one that is not so staid. This beautiful Church that makes progress....

Be positive, cultivate your spiritual life and, at the same time, go out, be capable of meeting people, especially those most despised and underprivileged. Do not be afraid of going out and swimming against the tide. Be both contemplatives and missionaries. Always keep Our Lady with you and please pray the rosary.... Do not neglect it! Always keep Our Lady with you at home, as did the apostle John. May she always accompany you and keep you.

ADDRESS TO SEMINARIANS AND NOVICES, PAUL VI
AUDIENCE HALL,
SATURDAY, JULY 6, 2013

FOR THE LOVE OF JESUS

Our Lady also wants to bring the great gift of Jesus to us, to us all; and with him she brings us his love, his peace, and his joy. In this, the Church is like Mary: the Church is not a shop, she is not a humanitarian agency, the Church is not an NGO [nongovernmental organization]. The church is sent to bring Christ and his gospel to all. She does not bring herself—whether small or great, strong or weak, the Church carries Jesus and should be like Mary when she went to visit Elizabeth. What did Mary take to her? Jesus. The Church brings Jesus: this is the center of the Church, to carry Jesus! If, as a hypothesis, the Church were not to bring Jesus, she would be a dead Church. The Church must bring Jesus, the love of Jesus, the charity of Jesus.

GENERAL AUDIENCE, ST. PETER'S SQUARE
WEDNESDAY, OCTOBER 23, 2013

SEEK NEW METHODS OF EVANGELIZATION

It is Christ who leads the Church through his Spirit. The Holy Spirit is the soul of the Church through his life-giving and unifying force: out of many, he makes one single body, the mystical body of Christ. Let us never yield to pessimism, to that bitterness that the devil offers us every day; let us not yield to pessimism or discouragement: let us be quite certain that the Holy Spirit bestows upon the Church, with his powerful breath, the courage to persevere and also to seek new methods of evangelization, so as to bring to Gospel to the uttermost ends of the earth (cf. Acts 1:8)....

I entrust my ministry and your ministry to the powerful intercession of Mary, our Mother, Mother of the Church. Under her maternal gaze, may each one of you continue gladly along your path, attentive to the voice of her divine Son, strengthening your unity, persevering in your common prayer and bearing witness to the true faith in the constant presence of the Lord. With these sentiments, which I really mean, I impart a heartfelt apostolic blessing, which I extend to your co-workers and to all those entrusted to your pastoral care.

ADDRESS TO THE COLLEGE OF CARDINALS,
CLEMENTINE HALL
FRIDAY, MARCH 15, 2013

IN THE FOOTSTEPS OF MARY

What joy I feel as I come to the house of the one of every Brazilian, the shrine of Our Lady of Aparecida! The day after my election as bishop of Rome, I visited the Basilica of St. Mary Major in Rome, in order to entrust my ministry to Our Lady. Today I have come here to ask Mary our Mother for the success of World Youth Day and to place at her feet the life of the people of Latin America.

There is something that I would like to say first of all. Six years ago the Fifth General Conference of the Bishops of Latin America and the Caribbean was held in this shrine. Something beautiful took place here, which I witnessed at first hand. I saw how the bishops—who were discussing the theme of encountering Christ, discipleship and mission—felt encouraged, supported and in some way inspired by the thousands of pilgrims who came here day after day to entrust their lives to Our Lady. That conference was a great moment of Church.

It can truly be said that the Aparecida document was born of this interplay between the labors of the bishops and the simple faith of the pilgrims, under Mary's maternal protection. When the Church looks for Jesus, she always knocks at his Mother's door and asks: "Show us Jesus." It is from Mary that the Church learns true discipleship. That is why the Church always goes out on mission in the footsteps of Mary.

Today, looking forward to the World Youth Day which has brought me to Brazil, I too come to knock on the door of the house of Mary—who loved and raised Jesus— that she may help all of us, pastors of God's people, parents and educators, to pass on to our young people the values that can help them build a nation and a world which are more just, united and fraternal.

HOMILY, SHRINE OF OUR LADY OF
APARECIDA, BRAZIL
WEDNESDAY, JULY 24, 2013

GIVE CREDIBLE WITNESS

This history of the first Christian community tells us something very important which applies to the Church in all times and also to us. When a person truly knows Jesus Christ and believes in him, that person experiences his presence in life as well as the power of his Resurrection and cannot but communicate this experience. And if this person meets with misunderstanding or adversity, he behaves like Jesus in his Passion: he answers with love and with the power of the truth.

In praying the Regina Coeli together, let us ask for the help of Mary Most Holy so that the church throughout the world may proclaim the Resurrection of the Lord with candor and courage and give credible witness to it with signs of brotherly love. Brotherly love is the closest testimony we can give that Jesus is alive with us, that Jesus is risen.

REGINA COELI, ST. PETER'S SQUARE
SUNDAY, APRIL 14, 2013

AN EXTRAORDINARY OUTPOURING
OF THE SPIRIT

The Feast of Pentecost commemorates the outpouring of the Holy Spirit on the apostles gathered in the Upper Room. Like Easter, this event took place on a pre-existing Jewish feast and ended with a surprise. The Acts of the Apostles describes the signs and fruits of that extraordinary outpouring: the strong wind and tongues of fire; fear disappeared, leaving courage in its place; tongues melted and everyone understood the message. Wherever the Spirit of God reaches, everything is reborn and transfigured....

We turn to the Virgin Mary, who on that Pentecost morning was in the Upper Room, the Mother with her children. In her, the force of the Holy Spirit truly accomplished "great things" (Luke 1:49). She herself said so. May she, the Mother of the Redeemer and Mother of the Church, obtain through her intercession a renewed outpouring of God's Spirit upon the Church and upon the world.

REGINA COELI, ST. PETER'S SQUARE
SUNDAY, JUNE 8, 2014, SOLEMNITY OF PENTECOST

A HOME FOR ALL PEOPLES

On this World Mission Day, my thoughts turn to all the local churches. Let us not be robbed of the joy of evangelization! I invite you to immerse yourself in the joy of the Gospel and nurture a love that can light up your vocation and your mission. I urge each of you to recall, as if you were making an interior pilgrimage, that "first love" with which the Lord Jesus Christ warmed your heart, not for the sake of nostalgia but in order to persevere in joy. The Lord's disciples persevere in joy when they sense his presence, do his will and share with others their faith, hope and evangelical charity.

Let us pray through the intercession of Mary, the model of humble and joyful evangelization, that the Church may become a welcoming home, a Mother for all peoples and the source of rebirth for our world.

MESSAGE FOR WORLD MISSION DAY,
FROM THE VATICAN
SUNDAY, JUNE 8, 2014

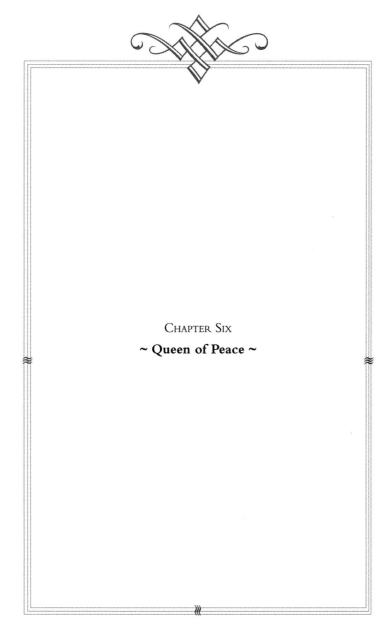

CHAPTER SIX

~ Queen of Peace ~

MARY, ICON OF PEACE

At the beginning of a new year, the Church invites us to contemplate Mary's divine maternity as an icon of peace. The ancient promise finds fulfillment in her person. She believed in the words of the angel, conceived her Son and thus became the Mother of the Lord. Through her, through her "yes," the fullness of time came about.

The Gospel we have just heard tells us that the Virgin Mary "treasured all these words and pondered them in her heart" (Luke 2:19). She appears to us as a vessel filled to the brim with the memory of Jesus, as the Seat of Wisdom to whom we can have recourse to understand his teaching aright. Today, Mary makes it possible for us to grasp the meaning of events which affect us personally, events which also affect our families, our countries and the entire world. Where philosophical reason and political negotiation cannot arrive, there the power of faith, which brings the grace of Christ's Gospel, can arrive, opening ever new pathways to reason and to negotiation.

HOMILY, VATICAN BASILICA,
FRIDAY, JANUARY 1, 2016, WORLD DAY OF PEACE

Pope Francis @Pontifex · September 2, 2013

We want a peaceful world, we want to be men and women of peace.

THE WAY OF PEACE

Today we celebrate the World Day of Peace, whose theme is: "Overcome Indifference and Win Peace."

Peace, which God the Father wants to sow in the world, must be cultivated by us. Not only this, but it must also be "won." This leads to a real struggle, a spiritual battle that takes place in our hearts. Because the enemy of peace is not only war, but also indifference, which makes us think only of ourselves and creates barriers, suspicions, fears, and closure. These things are enemies of peace. We have, thanks be to God, a great deal of information; but, at times, we are so overwhelmed by facts that we become distracted by reality, from the brother and sister who need us. Let us begin this year by opening our heart and calling attention to neighbors, to those who are near. This is the way to win peace.

May the queen of peace, the Mother of God, whose solemnity we celebrate today, help us with this.

ANGELUS, ST. PETER'S SQUARE,
FRIDAY, JANUARY 1, 2016, WORLD DAY OF PEACE

GRANT PEACE IN OUR DAY

May this gentle and loving Mother obtain for us the Lord's blessing upon the entire human family. On this, the World Day of Peace, we especially implore her intercession that the Lord may grant peace in our day; peace in hearts, peace in families, peace among the nations.... From every people, culture and religion, let us join our forces. May he guide and sustain us, who, in order to make us all brothers and sisters, became our servant.

Let us look to Mary, let us contemplate the Holy Mother of God.

HOMILY, VATICAN BASILICA
THURSDAY, JANUARY 1, 2015, WORLD DAY OF PEACE

Pope Francis @Pontifex · January 16, 2014
Let us pray for peace, and let us bring it about, starting in our own homes!

SEEKING A PEACEFUL EXISTENCE

Our Lady…is the Mother of every home, of every wounded family, of all who are seeking to return to a peaceful existence. Today we thank her for protecting the people of Sri Lanka from so many dangers, past and present. Mary never forgot her children on this resplendent island. Just as she never left the side of her Son on the Cross, so she never left the side of her suffering Sri Lankan children.

Today, we want to thank Our Lady for that presence. In the wake of so much hatred, violence and destruction, we want to thank her for continuing to bring us Jesus, who alone has the power to heal open wounds and to restore peace to broken hearts. But we also want to ask her to implore for us the grace of God's mercy. We ask also for the grace to make reparation for our sins and for all the evil which this land has known.…

Dear brothers and sisters, I am happy to be with you in Mary's house. Let us pray for one another. Above all, let us ask that this shrine may always be a house of prayer and a haven of peace. Through the intercession of Our Lady of Madhu, may all people find here inspiration and strength to build a future of reconciliation, justice and peace for all the children of this beloved land. Amen.

ADDRESS, SHRINE OF OUR LADY OF THE ROSARY,
MADHU, SRI LANKA
WEDNESDAY, JANUARY 14, 2015

Pope Francis @Pontifex · August 14, 2014
Mary, Queen of Peace, help us to root out hatred and live in harmony.

MAY WE BE HERALDS OF WORLD PEACE

At the end of our Mass, we turn once more to Our Lady, Queen of Heaven. To her we bring all our joys, our sorrows and our hopes.... On this day when Korea celebrates its liberation, we ask Our Lady to watch over this noble nation and its citizens. And we commend to her care all the young people who have joined us from throughout Asia. May they be joyful heralds of the dawn of a world of peace in accordance with God's gracious plan!

ANGELUS, DAEJEON, SOUTH KOREA
FRIDAY, AUGUST 15, 2014, FEAST OF THE ASSUMPTION

A THREEFOLD APPEAL

I would like to make a threefold appeal to the leaders of nations: to refrain from drawing other peoples into conflicts or wars which destroy not only their material, cultural and social legacy, but also—and in the long term—their moral and spiritual integrity; to forgive or manage in a sustainable way the international debt of the poorer nations; and, to adopt policies of cooperation which, instead of bowing before the dictatorship of certain ideologies, will respect the values of local populations and, in any case, not prove detrimental to the fundamental and inalienable right to life of the unborn.

I entrust these reflections, together with my best wishes for the New Year, to the intercession of the Blessed Virgin Mary, our Mother, who cares for the needs of our human family, that she may obtain from her Son Jesus, the Prince of Peace, the granting of our prayers and the blessing of our daily efforts for a fraternal and united world.

MESSAGE FOR THE WORLD DAY OF PEACE,
FROM THE VATICAN
TUESDAY, DECEMBER 8, 2015, SOLEMNITY OF
THE IMMACULATE CONCEPTION

THE DAWN OF PEACE

Yet at this moment in which we are praying intensely for peace, this word of the Lord touches us to the core, and essentially tells us: there is a more profound war that we must all fight! It is the firm and courageous decision to renounce evil and its enticements and to choose the good, ready to pay in person: this is following Christ, this is what taking up our cross means! This profound war against evil!…

Dear brothers and sisters, today we are also commemorating the Nativity of the Virgin Mary, a feast particularly dear to the Eastern churches. And let all of us now send a beautiful greeting to all the brothers, sisters, bishops, monks and nuns of the Eastern churches, both Orthodox and Catholic, a beautiful greeting! Jesus is the sun; Mary is the dawn that heralds his rising.

Yesterday evening we kept vigil, entrusting to her intercession our prayers for peace in the world, especially in Syria and throughout the Middle East. Let us now invoke her as Queen of Peace. Queen of Peace pray for us! Queen of Peace pray for us!

ANGELUS, ST. PETER'S SQUARE
SUNDAY, SEPTEMBER 8, 2013

HOPING AGAINST HOPE

On this pilgrimage, which was a true grace of the Lord, I wished to bring a word of hope, but I also received one in return! I received it from so many brothers and sisters who hope "against all hope" (Romans 4:18), amid such suffering, like those of one who has fled his own country because of the conflicts; like those of all who, in various parts of the world, are discriminated against and scorned on account of their faith in Christ. Let us continue to stay close to them! Let us pray for them and for peace in the Holy Land and throughout the Middle East. May the prayer of the whole Church also support the journey to full Christian unity, so that the world may believe in the love of God who in Jesus Christ came to dwell among us.

And I invite everyone now to pray together, to pray together to Our Lady, Queen of Peace, Queen of Christian unity, the *Mamma* of all Christians: that she may give peace to us, to the whole world, and that she may accompany us on this path of unity.

GENERAL AUDIENCE, ST. PETER'S SQUARE
WEDNESDAY, MAY 28, 2014

QUEEN OF PEACE, PRAY FOR US

I received with concern the news of the Christian communities in Mosul, Iraq, and in other parts of the Middle East, where they have lived from the beginning of Christianity with their fellow citizens, offering a meaningful contribution to the good of society. Today, they are persecuted; our brothers and sisters are persecuted, they are pushed out, forced to leave their homes without the opportunity to take anything with them. To these families and to these people I would like to express my closeness and my steadfast prayer....

May the God of peace create in all an authentic desire for dialogue and reconciliation. Violence is not conquered with violence. Violence is conquered with peace! Let us pray in silence, asking for peace; everyone, in silence.... Mary, queen of peace, pray for us!

ANGELUS, ST. PETER'S SQUARE
SUNDAY, JULY 20, 2014

Pope Francis @Pontifex · June 7, 2014
Prayer is all-powerful. Let us use it to bring peace to the Middle East and peace to the world. #weprayforpeace

Pope Francis @Pontifex · April 24, 2016

Dear young people, with the grace of God you can become authentic and courageous Christians, witnesses to love and peace.

THE FRUIT OF FAITH

Let us now invoke Mary, Queen of Peace. During her life on earth, she met many difficulties, related to the daily toils of life. But she never lost peace of heart, the fruit of faithful abandonment to God's mercy. Let us ask Mary, our gentle Mother, to show the entire world the sure way of love and peace.

ANGELUS, ST. PETER'S SQUARE
SUNDAY, JANUARY 4, 2015

WE ARE BUILDERS OF PEACE

Two roads intersect today: the Feast of Mary the Most Holy Mother of God and the World Day of Peace. Eight days ago the angelic proclamation rang out: "Glory to God and peace to all men." Today we welcome it anew from the Mother of Jesus, who "kept all these things, pondering them in her heart" (Luke 2:19), in order to make of it our commitment over the course of the year which has just commenced....

With filial trust, let us place our hopes in the hands of Mary, the Mother of the Redeemer. To she who extends her motherhood to all mankind, let us entrust the cry for peace of peoples who are oppressed by war and violence, so that the courage of dialogue and reconciliation might prevail over temptations to revenge, tyranny and corruption. Let us ask her to grant that the Gospel of fraternity, which the Church proclaims and to which she bears witness, may speak to every conscience and bring down the walls that prevent enemies from recognizing one another as brothers.

ANGELUS, ST. PETER'S SQUARE
WEDNESDAY, JANUARY 1, 2014, WORLD DAY OF PEACE

PROMOTING A CULTURE OF PEACE

In the next few days, various capital cities will commemorate the 70th anniversary of the end of the Second World War in Europe. On this occasion, I entrust to the Lord, by the intercession of Mary Queen of Peace, my hope that society may learn from the mistakes of the past and that, faced with the current conflicts that are tearing asunder various regions of the world, all civic leaders may persevere in their search for the common good and in the promotion of a culture of peace.

GENERAL AUDIENCE, ST. PETER'S SQUARE
WEDNESDAY, MAY 6, 2015

Pope Francis @Pontifex · January 27, 2015
Auschwitz cries out with the pain of immense suffering and pleads for a future of respect, peace and encounter among peoples.

FELLOWSHIP AND FRATERNITY

In this, my first message for the World Day of Peace, I wish to offer to everyone, individuals and peoples, my best wishes for a life filled with joy and hope. In the heart of every man and woman is the desire for a full life, including that irrepressible longing for fraternity which draws us to fellowship with others and enables us to see them not as enemies or rivals, but as brothers and sisters to be accepted and embraced....

May Mary, the Mother of Jesus, help us to understand and live every day the fraternity that springs up from the heart of her Son, so as to bring peace to each person on this our beloved earth.

MESSAGE FOR THE WORLD DAY OF PEACE,
FROM THE VATICAN
SUNDAY, DECEMBER 8, 2013

Pope Francis @Pontifex · August 14, 2014
Mary, Queen of Peace, help us to root out hatred and live in harmony.

A SONG FOR ALL HUMANITY

The exultation of the humble maiden of Galilee, expressed in the Canticle of the Magnificat, becomes the song of all humanity, which sees with satisfaction the Lord stoop over all men and all women, humble creatures, and assume them with him into heaven.

The Lord stoops over the humble to raise them up, as the Canticle of the Magnificat proclaims. This hymn of Mary also leads us to think of the many current painful situations, in particular of women overwhelmed by the burden of life and by the tragedy of violence, of women enslaved by the oppression of the powerful, of children forced into inhuman labor, of women obliged to surrender in body and in spirit to the greed of men.

May they begin as soon as possible a life of peace, of justice, of love, awaiting the day in which they will finally feel they are held by hands which do not humiliate them, but which lift them tenderly and lead them on the path of life, to heaven. May Mary, a maiden, a woman who suffered a great deal in her life, make us think of these women who suffer so much. Let us ask the Lord that he himself may take them by the hand and lead them on the path of life, freeing them from these forms of slavery.

Now let us turn trustingly to Mary, gentle sweet queen of heaven, and ask her: "Give us days of peace, watch over our journey, let us see your Son, filled with the joy of heaven" (Hymn of Second Vespers).

ANGELUS, ST. PETER'S SQUARE
MONDAY, AUGUST 15, 2016, FEAST OF THE ASSUMPTION

A PLEA FOR THE GIFT OF PEACE

In this, the birthplace of the Prince of Peace, I wish to invite you, President Mahmoud Abbas, together with President Shimon Peres, to join me in heartfelt prayer to God for the gift of peace. I offer my home in the Vatican as a place for this encounter of prayer.

All of us want peace. Many people build it day by day through small gestures and acts; many of them are suffering, yet patiently persevere in their efforts to be peacemakers. All of us—especially those placed at the service of their respective peoples—have the duty to become instruments and artisans of peace, especially by our prayers.

Building peace is difficult, but living without peace is a constant torment. The men and women of these lands, and of the entire world, all of them, ask us to bring before God their fervent hopes for peace....

As we prepare to conclude our celebration, our thoughts turn to Mary Most Holy, who here, in Bethlehem, gave birth to Jesus her Son. Our Lady is the one who, more than any other person, contemplated God in the human face of Jesus. Assisted by St. Joseph, she wrapped him in swaddling clothes and laid him in the manger.

To Mary we entrust this land and all who dwell here, that they may live in justice, peace and fraternity. We entrust also the pilgrims who come here to draw from the sources of the Christian faith—so many of them are also present at this Holy Mass.

Mary, watch over our families, our young people and our elderly. Watch over those who have lost faith and hope. Comfort the sick, the imprisoned and all who suffer. Watch over the Church's pastors and the entire community of believers; may they be "salt and light" in this blessed land....

We entrust the future of our human family to Mary Most Holy, that new horizons may open in our world, with the promise of fraternity, solidarity and peace.

REGINA COELI, BETHLEHEM
SUNDAY, MAY 25, 2014

MAKE US BUILDERS OF JUSTICE AND PEACE

The news from Iraq leaves us incredulous and alarmed: thousands of people, many Christians among them, are being driven from their homes in a brutal way; children are dying of thirst and hunger while fleeing; women abducted; people massacred; every type of violence; destruction everywhere; destruction of houses, of religious, historic and cultural heritage. Yet all of this grievously offends God and grievously offends humanity. Hatred is not borne in the name of God! War is not waged in the name of God! All of us, thinking about this situation, about these people, let us be silent now and pray....

In Gaza as well, after a ceasefire, war has broken out again, claiming innocent victims, children... and does nothing but worsen the conflict between the Israelis and Palestinians.

Let us pray together to the God of peace, through the intercession of the Virgin Mary: Grant peace, Lord, in our day, and make us builders of justice and peace. Mary, Queen of Peace, pray for us.

ANGELUS, ST. PETER'S SQUARE
SUNDAY, AUGUST 10, 2014

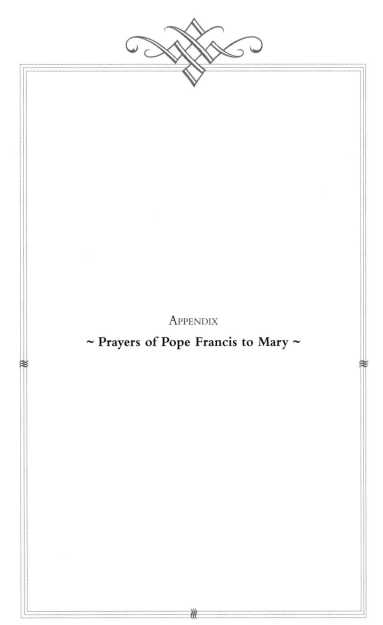

APPENDIX

~ **Prayers of Pope Francis to Mary** ~

MOTHER OF SILENCE

Mother of silence, who watches over the mystery of God,

Save us from the idolatry of the present time, to which those who forget are condemned.

Purify the eyes of pastors with the eye-wash of memory:

Take us back to the freshness of the origins, for a prayerful, penitent church.

Mother of the beauty that blossoms from faithfulness to daily work,

Lift us from the torpor of laziness, pettiness, and defeatism.

Clothe pastors in the compassion that unifies, that makes whole; let us discover the joy of a humble,

brotherly, serving Church.

Mother of tenderness who envelops us in patience and mercy,

Help us burn away the sadness, impatience and rigidity of those who do not know what it means to belong.

Intercede with your Son to obtain that our hands, our feet, our hearts be agile: let us build the Church with the truth of love.

Mother, we shall be the people of God, pilgrims bound for the kingdom. Amen.

—MAY 23, 2013

WOMAN OF LISTENING

Mary, woman of listening, open our ears; grant us to know how to listen to the word of your Son Jesus among the thousands of words of this world; grant that we may listen to the reality in which we live, to every person we encounter, especially those who are poor, in need, in hardship.

Mary, woman of decision, illuminate our mind and our heart, so that we may obey, unhesitating, the word of your Son Jesus; give us the courage to decide, not to let ourselves be dragged along, letting others direct our life.

Mary, woman of action, obtain that our hands and feet move "with haste" toward others, to bring them the charity and love of your Son Jesus, to bring the light of the Gospel to the world, as you did. Amen.

—MAY 31, 2013

MOTHER OF THE CHURCH AND
MOTHER OF OUR FAITH

Mother, help our faith!

Open our ears to hear God's word and to recognize his voice and call.

Awaken in us a desire to follow in his footsteps, to go forth from our own land and to receive his promise.

Help us to be touched by his love, that we may touch him in faith.

Help us to entrust ourselves fully to him and to believe in his love, especially at times of trial, beneath the

shadow of the cross, when our faith is called to mature.

Sow in our faith the joy of the Risen One.

Remind us that those who believe are never alone.

Teach us to see all things with the eyes of Jesus, that he may be light for our path. And may this light of

faith always increase in us, until the dawn of that undying day which is Christ himself, your Son, our

Lord!

—*LUMEN FIDEI,* JUNE 29, 2013

ACT OF CONSECRATION TO OUR LADY OF APARECIDA

Mary Most Holy by the merits of Our Lord Jesus Christ, in your beloved image of Aparecida, spread infinite favors over all Brazil.

I, unworthy to be counted among your sons and daughters but full of desire to share in the blessings of your mercy, lie prostrate at your feet. To you I consecrate my intentions, that they may ever dwell on the love that you merit; to you I consecrate my tongue that it may ever praise you and spread your devotion; to you I consecrate my heart, that, after God, I may love you above all things.

Receive me, incomparable Queen, you whom Christ Crucified gave to us as Mother, and count me among your blessed sons and daughters; take me under your protection; come to my aid in all my needs, both spiritual and temporal, and above all at the hour of my death.

Bless me, heavenly helper, and through your powerful intercession, give me strength in my weakness, so that, by serving you faithfully in this life, I may praise you, love you and give you thanks in heaven, for all eternity. Let it be!

—JULY 24, 2013

ACT OF ENTRUSTMENT TO MARY,
VIRGIN OF FATIMA

Blessed Virgin Mary of Fatima,
with renewed gratitude for your motherly presence
we join in the voice of all generations that call you blessed.

We celebrate in you the great works of God,
who never tires of lowering himself in mercy over humanity,
afflicted by evil and wounded by sin,
to heal and to save it.

Accept with the benevolence of a Mother
this act of entrustment that we make in faith today,
before this your image, beloved to us.

We are certain that each one of us is precious in your eyes
and that nothing in our hearts has estranged you.

May that we allow your sweet gaze
to reach us and the perpetual warmth of your smile.

Guard our life with your embrace:

bless and strengthen every desire for good;

give new life and nourishment to faith;

sustain and enlighten hope;

awaken and animate charity;

guide us all on the path to holiness.

Teach us your own special love for the little and the poor,

for the excluded and the suffering,

for sinners and the wounded of heart:

gather all people under your protection

and give us all to your beloved Son, our Lord Jesus.

Amen.

—OCTOBER 13, 2013

PRAYER TO THE BLESSED VIRGIN MARY

Mary, Virgin and Mother,

you who, moved by the Holy Spirit,

welcomed the word of life

in the depths of your humble faith:

as you gave yourself completely to the Eternal One,

help us to say our own "yes"

to the urgent call, as pressing as ever,

to proclaim the good news of Jesus.

Filled with Christ's presence,

you brought joy to John the Baptist,

making him exult in the womb of his mother.

Brimming over with joy,

you sang of the great things done by God.

Standing at the foot of the cross

with unyielding faith,

you received the joyful comfort of the resurrection,

and joined the disciples in awaiting the Spirit

so that the evangelizing Church might be born.

Obtain for us now a new ardor born of the resurrection,

that we may bring to all the Gospel of life

which triumphs over death.

Give us a holy courage to seek new paths,

that the gift of unfading beauty
may reach every man and woman.

Virgin of listening and contemplation,
Mother of love, Bride of the eternal wedding feast,
pray for the Church, whose pure icon you are,
that she may never be closed in on herself
or lose her passion for establishing God's kingdom.

Star of the new evangelization,
help us to bear radiant witness to communion,
service, ardent and generous faith,
justice and love of the poor,
that the joy of the Gospel
may reach to the ends of the earth,
illuminating even the fringes of our world.

Mother of the living Gospel,
wellspring of happiness for God's little ones,
pray for us.

Amen. Alleluia!

—*EVANGELII GAUDIUM*, NOVEMBER 24, 2013

PRAYER TO THE IMMACULATE

Virgin most holy and immaculate,

to you, the honor of our people,

and the loving protector of our city,

do we turn with loving trust.

You are all-beautiful, O Mary!

In you there is no sin.

Awaken in all of us a renewed desire for holiness:

May the splendor of truth shine forth in our words,

the song of charity resound in our works,

purity and chastity abide in our hearts and bodies,

and the full beauty of the Gospel be evident in our lives.

You are all-beautiful, O Mary!

In you the Word of God became flesh.

Help us always to heed the Lord's voice:

May we never be indifferent to the cry of the poor,

or untouched by the sufferings of the sick and those in
       need;

may we be sensitive to the loneliness of the elderly and the
       vulnerability of children,

and always love and cherish the life of every human being.

You are all-beautiful, O Mary!

In you is the fullness of joy born of life with God.

Help us never to forget the meaning of our earthly journey:

May the kindly light of faith illumine our days,

the comforting power of hope direct our steps,

the contagious warmth of love stir our hearts;

and may our gaze be fixed on God, in whom true joy is

found.

You are all-beautiful, O Mary!

Hear our prayer; graciously hear our plea:

May the beauty of God's merciful love in Jesus abide in

our hearts,

and may this divine beauty save us, our city and the entire

world.

Amen.

—DECEMBER 8, 2013

ACT OF VENERATION TO THE IMMACULATE CONCEPTION

Mary our Mother,

Today the people of God celebrate, they venerate you, the Immaculate, ever preserved from the stain of sin.

Accept the homage I offer you in the name of the Church in Rome and throughout the world.

Knowing that you, our Mother, are totally free from sin is a consolation to us.

Knowing that evil has no power over you fills us with hope and strength in our daily struggle against the threat of the evil one.

But in this struggle we are not alone, we are not orphans, for Jesus, before dying on the cross, gave you to us as our Mother.

Though we are sinners, we are still your children, the children of the Immaculate, called to that holiness that has shown resplendent in you by the grace of God from the beginning.

Inspired by this hope, today we invoke your motherly protection for us, our families, this city and the world.

Through your intercession, may the power of God's love that preserved you from original sin, free humanity from every form of spiritual and material slavery and make God's plan of salvation victorious in hearts and in history.

May grace prevail over pride in us, too, your children.

May we become merciful as our heavenly Father is merciful.

In this time leading up to the celebration of Jesus's birth, teach us to go against the current: to strip ourselves, to be humble, and giving, to listen and be silent, to go out of ourselves, granting space to the beauty of God, the source of true joy.

Pray for us, our Immaculate Mother!

—DECEMBER 8, 2014

PRAYER TO THE "VIRGEN DE LA CARIDAD"

Our Lady of Charity of El Cobre,

Patroness of Cuba!

Hail, Mary,

full of grace!

You are the beloved Daughter of the Father,

Mother of Christ, our God,

the living Temple

of the Holy Spirit.

You carry in your name,

Virgin of Charity,

the memory of God who is Love,

the memory of the new commandments of Jesus,

the evocation of the Holy Spirit:

love poured into our hearts,

the fire of charity

sent on Pentecost

upon the Church,

the gift of the full freedom

of the children of God.

Blessed are you among women

and blessed is the fruit

of your womb, Jesus!

You came to visit our people
and you chose to remain with us
as Mother and Lady of Cuba,
on our pilgrimage
through the paths of history.

Your name and your image
are carved
into the hearts and minds
of all Cubans,
both in the country and abroad,
as a sign of hope
and the center of brotherly communion.
Holy Mary, Mother of God
and our Mother!

Pray for us
before your Son Jesus Christ,
intercede for us
with your motherly heart,
flooded with the love of the Holy Spirit.
Increase our faith,
awaken our hope,
broaden and strengthen our love.

Watch over our families,

protect our young people and our children,

console those who suffer.

Be the mother of the faithful

and of the pastors of the Church,

model and star of the new evangelization.

Mother of reconciliation!

Gather your people

scattered around the earth.

Make of our Cuban nation

a house of brothers and sisters

that this people may open wide

her mind, her heart

and her life to Christ,

the one Savior and Redeemer,

who lives and reigns with the Father

and the Holy Spirit

forever and ever.

Amen.

—SEPTEMBER 21, 2015